FAMILY STORIES

by Sharon Hacker

RoseDog Books
PITTSBURGH, PENNSYLVANIA 15238

RoseDog Books
585 Alpha Drive, Suite 103
Pittsburgh, PA 15238
Visit our website at www. rosedogbookstore. com

ISBN: 979-8-88527-937-6
eISBN: 979-8-88527-985-7

FAMILY STORIES

In years gone by you could take the country road Highway 13, also called the Little Thrill Hills. Driving a manual also called a Stick Shift kind of car for best results you would begin at the south end of Bethany MO. Following a more or less straight but hilly 2 lane country highway with farmlands on either side and all outlined in hedgerows full of trees and wild flowers and a multitude of edible vegetation. You would find blackberries and gooseberries in spring, nettles (ouch! But delicious wilted and packed with bacon bits) and mints and clover and rarely, mushrooms. These little pockets of natural growth were valuable cover for pheasants and quails to build their nests and lay their eggs. There were also fox dens here and there for the hunting needs of their little families. Birds chirping overhead. A mild breeze rifling through your hair as you drive with the windows open. Then coming to the first little hill, the trick is to hit the gas pedal just before you get to the top. If you have timed it just right the whole car goes airborne for a second or so, all 4 tires bouncing back to the pavement on the other side of that crest. It makes your tummy flutter.

How I would love one more drive down that road!

Continuing south you pass through Coffey which used to have about 100 people living there all lined up along 13. More little thrill hills, though the best ones are north of Coffey, soon enough you come out on the north side of Gallatin. If you kept going down 13 you would pass through truly beautiful farmland, old remains of Civil War houses now in ruins, and come out at Braymer. And Braymer, just so you know, was the place where Mormons were killed and the reason Missouri is still a hate word to some of that community in Salt Lake City.

But let's say you just end your trip at Gallatin. These days that would take about half an hour. It would have taken longer in 1883 because horse and carriage would have been the best way to get there.

In 1883 my grandfather Sam Hacker b 1868 was 15 years old. His father Sam Hacker b 1827 was a farmer outside Bethany, and a big James fan. I don't have any stories that either of my direct ancestors attended the Frank James trial in Gallatin in 1883 but they would certainly have known all about it. Small towns and rural communities are rightly famous for "good news travels fast" or the more correct version of that, gossip runs through the place so fast it hardly slows down to the speed of light.

There was a murder at Winston in 1881. My family owned the land (the old Ghoul farm) where the James gang hid their horses under the stone works that supported the train tracks, the place where the shooting happened. And the train passengers were robbed at that time.

Jesse James was shot at his home in St. Joseph in 1882. His older brother Frank then gave himself up to the governor and stood trial,

State of Missouri vs Frank James at Gallatin, county seat of Daviess County where Winston is located. The courthouse in the center of the town square couldn't hold the crowds so the trial was held at an opera house that I don't know. Maybe it still stands but is called something else by now. More likely it's gone.

Anyway it was the trial of the century at least among the locals. It was like a tent carnival set up all around the square, with items for purchase including snake oil remedies. At least one of the witnesses who testified at the trial was drunk when he took the stand. There were reporters galore covering that story. At the end, Frank was acquitted of the charge of murder during that Winston train robbery. The victim was a railroad conductor who was recognised by Jesse as having been a railroad conductor near the scene of a shootout of the Samuel farm at Kearney a few years before that. Their little brother had been killed in that gun battle but Frank and Jesse had escaped. So when they met again, the east side of Winston, that conductor was shot in the back many times as he was getting down the stairs to leave the train. But maybe Frank wasn't the one who did it.

This was the setting and the circumstances of that town in the last years of the 1800's. It seems like an old Western movie set but no, it really is an entire little village that was once kind of a booming town. But full of James fans though there must also have been people who didn't enjoy getting their life savings stolen.

Sam Hacker b 1868 grew up and married Minnie Caledonia Kelley about 1890, and farmed around Bethany and Gallatin for many years. But between times the couple with their children took a covered wagon trip to a 160 acre homestead they were interested in owning. The deal was for the cost to be paid in labor. So they were to go to a certain place, put up a house, and work that land for 5 years.

If they could stay there the whole time, the property would be deeded over to them. Their homestead was outside Temple, Oklahoma Territory in Cotton County near the Red River which forms the border with Texas. Just up the road from them, Fort Lawton where my sister's husband Enoch Brewer was once stationed, but in the early part of the 1900's it was where Geronimo was kept in prison.

My father was born on that Temple homestead on 11 July 1906 the year before Oklahoma became a state. He was the first person in his straight line to be born outside the United States in at least 100 years. He was the 7th of 9 children. The family disagreed about what to name him so the top 3 names were all given to him; Clarence Olin Dean Hacker. This seems like a very welcome baby into their little Oklahoma (probably sod house) homestead. But crops don't grow the same in Oklahoma as they do in Missouri so it wasn't long before the family turned back to Bethany. That's over 500 miles but these days you could drive it in less than 8 hours. In the year they made that trip, would have taken some weeks, maybe at 12 miles a day. In a covered wagon 4 feet wide by 6 feet long the belongings were stacked and carried. Grandpa up front driving the horse, Grandma beside him with a baby on her lap and maybe a toddler between the parents, the other children walking along beside the wagon. Oh, and their little rat terrier, beloved dog. At nights they might sleep in the wagon or else under it if the night was too hot

The older children were Bessie, Janie, Charlie, Roy, and Nora. There was also a baby Maggie who didn't survive infancy but I can't find out the exact birth order. Anyway, Clarence was the 7th child.

While they lived at Temple, Grandma (Minnie (Kelley) Hacker) had a cowboy confrontation. Some men rode up to the homestead. They were carrying torches. This was once Grandpa had left the house and was working a far field. Thinking no doubt, the little woman and her children inside were the least likely to give them any grief, they intended to burn that house down.

Grandma came out to meet them with a shotgun and that little rat terrier. She said, "Get off my land before I put a hole through you big enough for my dog to jump through." And they believed her. They left. It's worth noting that most people did believe Grandma. She didn't ever threaten. She did warn them, however. If she had not been believed she was prepared to back up those words. My dad was like that, too.

At the time that happened there was a lot of resentment against homesteaders. Tribes from all over the country had been relocated to Oklahoma Territory, which formerly was called Indian Territory. And then people came in to take even that land from them. Cattle ranchers also had been in the habit of grazing their cattle all over the place but then homesteaders came in and put up barbed wire fences which upset the whole economics previously in place. So of course there were tensions between all these groups. The cowboys were the only ones who tried to harm my people. As for the various tribes in the area, once Geronimo had been captured the attacks on isolated homes stopped.

The whole thing came to nothing for Sam Hacker. He was not able to get crops to grow and for that reason they couldn't stay on that land for 5 years. So it was, probably by harvest time, that they packed everything back into that covered wagon that had brought them there and returned to Bethany.

Sam Hacker b 1868 had 7 older siblings and only 1 younger brother. His oldest brother Dan was the car dealer in Bethany. It seems odd that such a luxury item would be in enough demand that an entire business could be supported by selling cars. All brands of cars.

So Bethany was a prosperous enough place and Dan Hacker was the perfect age to get involved in this latest fad. Many people thought this crazy idea of a horseless carriage would just lose its attraction and soon be completely forgotten. They called it a fad because other things have come into a time of being wanted, sooner or later falling out of favor as people found other things more interesting. In the matter of cars, such sound thinking was completely out of touch. So far cars are as popular today as they were more than a century ago.

It would be interesting to see what top companies in the stock market were doing in 1906. Are any of them still in existence? Well, Walgreen's, and Harley Davidson, and maybe more that I can't think of. But nobody uses the telegraph any more. We do use phones but nothing like what was the standard Bell telephone system of those years. No more plug-in switchboards to connect callers.

So there were some pretty adequate farms around Bethany. There were some churches and schools and shops where people could buy or sell their items. None of that was true of Temple. But it was still hard for him to give up his dream of going west and finding his own prosperity there. Grandpa had other skills besides farming. He did carpentry so finding work was never a problem for him. He just wanted to do what all the newspapers were urging young people to do by moving "out west" as it was called.

Wyatt Earp was still alive then. He had been the marshall at Dodge, Kansas. With Doc Holliday and that whole overworked story of the shootout at the OK Coral, it seems hard to imagine that this very midwestern strip of Tornado Alley was the wild west of grandpa's youth. Bethany must have seemed much more settled by contrast.

Anyway, the family walked and rode the weeks it took to get from Temple, OK back to Bethany. But soon they took off again to go to

New Mexico. John Calvin Hacker, one of the older brothers, had done the homestead work there, and had been able to stay on the land ever since. So Sam and Minnie and now 7 children made another covered wagon trip. This time they went to an area near Tucumcari in a place they just called Mexico. No doubt that also was a territory at the time.

There they set up another homestead. A rattlesnake got into position to strike my aunt Nora when she was a little girl playing at some distance from the rest of the family. That little rat terrier saw the whole thing. He jumped on that snake and killed it before it could bite her, but he was bitten. The family gave him a dose of turpentine, of all things, and stayed up with him through the long hours until he recovered. I have heard that they also used turpentine on themselves though more often they used wild plants for their medical needs. The whole thing turned out ok, the dog recovered, though I don't know why his name has been left out of these stories. They always just called him the little rat terrier so it's possible they didn't give him a name.

At that New Mexico homestead another little boy was born. This was my Uncle Walter, probably Daddy's best friend of his whole life

And two of the older girls died there. One was Maggie and she just was found unresponsive one morning. The other was Bessie.

Bessie was remembered as the smart one of the family. She told her father, "For God's sake Dad, let's get out of this God forsaken place before one of us dies!" But he was stubborn and refused to give it up at that time

Then came a time when water flowing through their property became contaminated. Water borne illnesses have been around probably always. But more or less invisible. The oldest 3 girls were Bessie, Janie, and Nora and all 3 of them had diphtheria. Two of them recovered from it. Bessie did not.

Other people around them had to have had diphtheria as well. They were quarantined. People brought boxes of food for them but left it far from the house for fear of contagion. Maybe they didn't connect the whole thing to the water. Anyway, it was believed that diphtheria was contagious. When Bessie died, her parents had to bury her themselves. What an awful thing! Especially since every surviving member of the family remembered what she said about one of them dying, and then she was the one who died.

But this is when they left. Back on that covered wagon trip back to Bethany.

Grandpa driving the horse, Grandma sitting beside him. This time definitely holding baby Walter with baby Clarence sitting between his parents, the 4 older children that had survived walking beside the wagon (that would be Aunt Janie, Aunt Nora, Uncle Charlie, and Uncle Roy). They were leaving two little girls behind them. I can't even think of how that must have felt! When of a sudden they noticed 3 men on horses, of an unknown tribe. Those men approached them and rode alongside, trying to talk to them.

Language kept them from understanding each other. But the Indians gestured in such a way that their meaning was clear. They wanted one of those baby boys. My dad said they wanted Uncle Walter because he had such beautiful brown eyes. But Aunt Nora who was older, said they wanted my dad. I tend to take her word for it just because she was older. But it could have been either way.

Grandpa just kept driving but he shook his head. "No" must have been clearly stated. So they made an offer to trade a horse for a child. Again, No. So they offered more horses. Still, Grandpa kept driving, kept shaking his head, all the other children crawled up into the covered wagon, and everybody kind of held their breath. Grandma was clutching both babies tightly. None of them spoke. The Indians kept pace with them as they drove along. They stayed alongside for a long time, never giving up their intention to trade for one of those children. But after a long time passed, they turned away and left the family to continue on their journey

What I have always thought about that story, how pitiful must it be when someone needs a baby that badly. Maybe that tribe had taken so many losses and faced so many challenges that survival itself was a struggle. Yet, it seems they could have overpowered this little family and just taken whatever they wanted. They didn't do that. Instead, they tried to trade what was valuable to them and to most anyone else out on the prairie, a horse was actually a very worthwhile thing to own. So, they offered something that would have been an expensive trade.

Also I think if this family had been part of a whole wagon train instead of lone travellers, there most likely would have been a gun battle.

For the family's point of view, all but the babies knew how to use a gun, and they certainly had guns with them. Mostly hunting for their meals along the way, a gun would have been something any one of them could have put their hands on. Yet none of them did that. They were all really scared but nobody resorted to force.

What they did was to carry on a sort of communication where everybody knew what everybody else had to say. Eventually, each party went their separate ways.

And for a bunch of people who might have been highly prejudiced I give them the honor of having done the right thing even under such a trying circumstance as that.

(Oklahoma Territory had been called Indian Territory. Temple was in the tribal homelands of Apache and Commanche tribes but ever since the Andrew Jackson presidency other tribes had been relocated to reservations throughout the territory, why it was called Indian Territory. So the Atlantic coast tribes who had no similar language or even hunting skills were marched all the way west as their homelands became absorbed into the United States. It was a shoddy response to the challenges of such different groups of people moving into indigenous territories. So it was, once in Oklahoma, that these tribes were at a disadvantage among the tribes who already lived there, but unable to communicate with each other.)

By 1911 the family was living on a farm outside Bethany. The last child was born there. That was Aunt Marjorie. So if you look at statistics you will see that she and her older siblings and her father, if not the whole rest of that enormous family, came from Bethany, MO in Harrison County just on the Iowa border. What you wouldn't find is that 2 little boys were born and 2 little girls were buried outside the United States. By about the time Henry Ford really got his company going. The Spanish flu and World War 1 were still a few years in the future.

The house outside Bethany where the family lived was a nice Victorian kind of house. It had a front parlour where guests would be entertained. The nicest furniture they owned was in that parlour. When people came to visit, they didn't go to other rooms in the house but always were met in the parlour. A piano was there, and Aunt Janie was given piano lessons. She was then supposed to teach her brothers and sisters what she knew, but they soon showed her she wasn't the boss of them. Aunt Nora was the more bossy of all those children. But Aunt Janie would play the piano for their guests. Later on she would entertain her young gentleman friends in the parlour, with the whole rest of the family in there with them. The Hacker family was considered well-to-do by standards of the time. They had a middle class kind of house, furniture, and significant appliances but that standard of living was entirely based on hard work. There were lots of children who each had a share of the work to be done. No household servants were hired and also, in the times before the Civil War, no slaves were owned, at least not in a straight line to me all the way back to Merry Webb and Charles Burns, Sr. in Scotland.

Though electricity wasn't widely available, some people did have a telephone in the home. I don't know if any of Bethany were that prosperous, but certainly there was no phone in the home where Daddy grew up.

At the back of the first floor was the kitchen. There was a pantry beside it, an entire room where supplies were kept. Another room on the first floor was the family living room, where they all spent their evenings when there were no visitors. The children played in that room. Their father read and he talked with them. Their mother crocheted and did sewing repairs and she talked with them, too. At bedtime they all went upstairs to their little cots. The boys shared one bedroom, the girls shared one room, the parents had one room, though none of those were large rooms. They had furniture to hold their clothing because there were no closets in that house. And anyway, nobody had a lot of clothes. Maybe two or three full outfits, something to sleep in, something to wear to church or fancy occasions like a wedding, and something to do their usual work in. There may have been 2 sets of working clothes because laundry was a big production in those wringer washer years where clothes were hung outside on the clothesline to dry after going through all the wash cycles done manually. So for a house full of people, that job of laundry took a full day to do. Typically laundry was done on Monday. Ironing those clothes was left for Tuesday, again taking the whole day.

Wednesday was for washing the windows and waxing the furniture but that didn't take all day. Still, that was a lot of work. Thursday was the day to bake in quantity, again taking most of the day. Friday was for general cleaning of the whole house and getting everybody bathed and dressed and ready for Sunday. I don't know that they had a Saturday routine. Maybe they took a little down time of their own just to keep up their strength.

Outside there was a series of boards laid next to each other in a sort of sidewalk made of wood. It was typical for that area in the nicer homes, so that people could better keep themselves out of the mud coming and going from the house. Because again, laundry was such a concern.

One spooky night the family were telling scary stories right before bedtime. Sometime later in that night they woke up hearing an awful noise outside. My dad thought of ghosts right away. Upon investigation that scary noise turned out to be a cow who had come out of the barn and was walking on those boards. Cows weigh a lot and they don't walk daintily. Boards knock against each other, I can imagine what a child would fear after a night of scary stories, then to be awakened to such unusual sounds. But they all had a good laugh when the cause of it was discovered.

Behind the house there was a guest house. It probably only had a sitting room and a bedroom because no guest would be asked to do their own cooking. It also had its own private outhouse. The family used the regular outhouse. Now we are getting to subjects I don't like to remember since this much of my dad's childhood was also part of my childhood.

Still, people have always had to deal with such things and their way was to have all that waste material in a small building apart from the house. A Sears catalog was to be found on the floor, the actual stall was just a bench with a hole in it, sometimes those had 2 holes but usually only 1. Then a person would tear out black and white pages of the catalog to use for toilet paper. Everybody hated when the catalog got down to nothing but color pages because those hurt so bad. I don't know when toilet paper came into being but, simple though that is, it made such a difference to everyone's lives!

(I learned from working at Westvaco that toilet paper is made from waste paper that was originally white. Maybe it had lines, maybe not. When somebody makes mistakes on paper, they just toss out that paper. In an office, there is a lot of that kind of waste. And that is the stuff that gets shredded, compacted, diluted with water, then rolled thin to become the softer version of a Sears catalog, taking care of something vital and never going to go obsolete need that all people share.)

In that guest house in the back Grandma's mother ,(Jane Snead, widow of William Patterson Kelley) came a few times to stay for a while. That was Malinda Jane Snead, the grandma that Daddy called Grandma Snead though I would have thought he would call her Grandma Kelley. Maybe she took back her maiden name after the death of her husband when my Grandma Hacker was a little girl. I know that she was married to William Patterson Kelley, and that they lived at the first on her father's farm in Illinois straight east of St. Louis. He would have been Civil War soldier age but I haven't found any documentation on that in fact on Ancestry.com he isn't found at all, which I take for a good sign. I would just say on that subject, nobody in this country in the middle of the 1800's was neutral on any of the issues of that war. Still, I won't speculate on that subject. Maybe later I will pick back up with researching this Irish ancestry line. It needs to be done in the way I did it when I first started, by going to genealogy reading rooms for background information, and at the library for reading microfiche records.

That farm outside Bethany was located next to the farm owned by Sam Hacker's older brother Dan Hacker where he lived with his wife and two children. Because he hadn't married until his car dealership business had taken shape, his wife was much younger than he was. There were nearly 20 years between the ages of Sam Hacker and Dan Hacker, yet Sam Hacker had children quite a bit older than those of Dan Hacker. They were a boy and a girl and they were nearly the same age as Clarence. Besides which, their mother was my dad's favorite aunt. I can't recall any of their names but only the things he told me about them.

He would go out his kitchen door to the backyard, then cut through a field and come out at the back door of these little cousins. Without telling his mother anything of his plans, he would go over to play at their house. He loved doing that! He enjoyed being with them. But his good times came to an end when the two mothers got talking about him. His own mother learned he'd been going to visit the cousins, never letting her know where he was going, and so he had to stop.

I think he must have been comfortable in their home with only 2 other children living there. In his own home he was surrounded by siblings and most of them were older so didn't share his interests. But by not letting his mother know where he was going, that was against the rules. That was how it had to end.

When I was in high school someone called on the phone for me at school. I was called into the office to take the call. It was some lady asking me all kinds of personal questions about my father. What was his entire name, who were his parents, where was he born, and then she told me she was his cousin. She had been trying unsuccessfully to find him to let him know that her mother had passed away. She wanted me to tell him the funeral arrangements and ask if he would like to attend. That night when Daddy got home from work and we were all having our supper around the dinner table, I told the story of the phone call of that day. Daddy's face grew extra white when I said it was all about him. But when he heard it was his cousin who called, he was glad I'd given her the information. That's the first time he ever told the story of that favorite aunt and how he would go to play with those cousins, such details that were once important to him but he hadn't told me before that day. Maybe this was 1959 or 1960.

Anyway we all got dressed up in our best and went to that funeral in Bethany. There I heard more about her. How she'd been active in charities all her long widowhood, since her husband had died in the 1930's. I said that day that I would have liked to know her.

After the funeral we went to their family home which was right inside the town and not on a farm outside as I had expected. It was a fine Victorian kiind of place and all the dark wood furniture was quite tall. There was a low level of light inside because of how the windows were set so high in the walls, and they had ferns growing in pots. Daddy talked a long time with his cousin and my mother, my brother Paul, and I listened. It seemed he still got along very well with this cousin who was so close to his own age

Then we drove home to Winston. We took 13 south to Gallatin then the 12 miles further that we had to go to get to our house. These days you could take 35 and get there inside a half hour but that trip took us quite a bit longer. Daddy was usually happy to take the thrill hills at a good clip but of course that day we were all subdued. And he told how his Uncle Dan had started as a car dealer, then later sold only Fords, that when he died in the 1930's he was a very old man. I figure he must have been in his 80's or 90's and his wife may only have been about the age of my grandmother so 50's or 60'. Anyway, he left in his will a million dollars, to split 3 ways between his wife and children. Apparently they continued living in that same house that I had just been inside, and I assumed that the son had also died sometime earlier than his mother. They must have sold the business when Dan Hacker passed away

This Dan Hacker was the oldest child of Sam Hacker b 1827 and Catherine Ann (Pottorff) Hacker. My grandpa Sam Hacker b 1868 was their 8th of 9 children so nearly 20 years younger than his oldest brother.

The 1800's was and remains a century apart from all others. One of the many differences of that century was the practice of naming their children. This Dan Hacker was named for his paternal grandfather, the first Dan Hacker who was named for Daniel Boone as were many other boys around 1802. By naming the first boy after his paternal grandfather it was showing honor to that ancestor. The second son would be named after his maternal grandfather, and then a series of respected uncles and so on, then maybe some famous person or a name out of the Bible, and if there were enough sons, eventually a boy would be named for his own father. This is how my grandfather came to his name. Also they didn't use Senior and Junior but each wore that same name, often living right down the road from each other. I imagine there may have been some mixed up mail delivered in those years. The best way to tell one from another is to include the birth year. But for Dan Hacker, there was no question of which one he was. His grandfather Dan Hacker had died in 1850, he wasn't born until 1852, and soon after his birth most of the Burnsville, IN family moved to the northwestern part of Missouri and across the state line in the southwestern part of Iowa. Many of the descendants of that migration have stayed in that same place all this while.

It would be well to mention that Nancy (Burns) Hacker, the widow of the first Dan Hacker d 1850, lived on a farm and paid taxes on it in 1876, when she would have been 72 years old. Pretty tough work for that age, good thing lots of her sons and grandsons lived all around her outside of Bethany! That was the last record I could find of her until someone went physically looking for traces of her. I had said in the 1990's that she was in death as in life, somewhere near her people. Since my great grandfather Samuel Hacker b 1827 was one of her people, I hoped she might have been buried at the former Christian Church Cemetery in Bethany. Samuel Hacker b 1827, his wife Catherine Ann (Pottorff) Hacker, and their grandson Walter Hacker are buried next to each other in that cemetery. But Nancy Hacker isn't there. After more actual going to cemeteries just over the Iowa border, she was found. Mt. Ayr, IA is just a little way north of Bethany, MO. In that cemetery she's near to some of her descendants who didn't live to grow up. I was right about where she would be found, though I didn't know the actual location, still that is where she would want to be buried.

I should say, the oldest sons of those families, the ones who would have inherited their own family farm. We were never among the older children who inherited land so, when the land couldn't support any more generations, the younger children had to move into locations where they might be able to take care of their own families. As farm families of that century and possibly before that time, the typical farm family would include many children and most of those would live to grow up. (Though not all did, of course.) Their mothers married young, worked alongside their husbands and still had a baby nearly every year until into their mid forties. So 10 children was more the typical size of farm families, though city families would hardly be able to afford that many. There is a luxury of sorts to owning your own business (farming) and living where you work, with constant access to the top quality food products. Almost everything they needed could be had right out their own back door. Or else made from materials easy to find, or else sharing outgrown baby furniture with others of the family, or such as that. For anything else, they could either get it, make it, or live without it. Extremely self sufficient, hardy, no doctor visiting kind of hard working people.

A word about that first Dan Hacker b 1802. He was born the year that Lewis and Clark set off to explore the continent. His father was John Hacker b 1868. His mother was Massie (Spread) Hacker. Dan Hacker b 1802 married Nancy (Burns) Hacker b 1804 when they all lived in Clay County, KY where their fathers had been given land instead of military pay for their Revolutionary War service.(John Hacker was too young for that war but he fought the next one, which involved Little Turtle and the Miami tribe in northern Indiana; got badly beaten in that one by the way.) Nancy's paternal grandfather William Burns had fought in the Revolution, and Nancy's father was named Brice in honor of the commanding officer Brice Clark of that war. So Burns and Hackers and many of their relatives relocated to southern Indiana where Brice Burns platted the town of Burnsville. (The Hackers and the Burns ancestors of those times would have heard an earthquake that happened straight west of them, at New Madrid, MO. In 1811 and 1812 there were a series of earthquakes but the really big one was so big that it was heard hundreds of miles away. Dan Hacker and Nancy Burns would have been children then.)

There they met the Pottorff family and others connected to them, all of which had moved into Indiana from the Pennsylvania farmland near to Reading, PA. Anyway, by 1850 Burnsville was mostly full of family of one or other of those families. That was the year that Dan Hacker died of tuberculosis. Also in 1850 George Pottorff died in Burnsville, and Massie (Spread) Hacker died still living in Clay County, KY on the farm next to her youngest son. Also that same year Nancy (Burns) Hacker had grown children as well as 3 still young ones living at home, and she paid $5000 cash for a piece of property outside Burnsville, I believe it was a mill of some sort. Because it wasn't a very large piece of property, yet she paid more for that than her father had paid for the entire land that became Burnsville. Sam Hacker b 1827 married George Pottorff's granddaughter Catherine Ann Pottorff the day before her 19th birthday, in her parents' home. They were Ninevah Pottorff and Nancy (Allhands) Pottorff.

The main point I'm making here is that the memory of Dan Hacker was honored by passing it to a child, and that Dan Hacker was born into enormous boom times. People were moving. Goods were more widely available to the farther areas due to the big push of canal building that had just finished. Prosperity was to be expected. Maybe this is where the American Dream took shape. Charming little agricultural towns with a fine opera hall, where celebrities performed and also luxury goods for sale in their own ma and pa retail shops. I really don't have any more information on the Ford dealership owner Dan Hacker but I believe he may have grown up expecting to do well for himself. And when cars came into mid America he was the perfect age to get started in what many people thought was a passing fad. Anyway it turned out well for him.

THE DAY AT THE CIRCUS

As a little boy Clarence must have been a healthy, hearty child. He loved to go fishing and he knew a place where he could get down on the ground on his stomach, and reach both his hands into the stream of water. This was possibly a little creek on the farm outside Bethany. Maybe not his family farm, but a place known to him, and it seems to have been somewhere he went whenever he wanted to go fishing.

With his arms full out in front, and nothing holding him onto the bank except for the weight of his body, he would stick his hands into the water and then into a little opening in the bank. A sort of cave for fish and other creatures. The idea was to use just his hands to find a fish, take hold of their middle section, and sort of tickle their tummy, and this way grab and land a fish. He had done this successfully so he kept on doing it.

But one day while he was at that fishing spot, something took hold of his fingers and started pulling on him. What a reversal of that sport! He had a hard time getting free from that grip but once he was out of danger, he just left that place and never did that fishing by hand trick again. He had no idea what grabbed him but he clearly knew what almost happened to him.

Usually, though, once chores were done, Clarence and his brother Walter would explore their surroundings together.

Across the road from their house was an open field. One day there were people on that field, and the two boys went to see what that was all about. It turned out to be a traveling circus. Since about the time of the Civil War there had been small circuses traveling around the small towns of rural America. The idea was to set up a tent venue and put on one performance that evening, then pack it all up and go on down the road to the next town where they would do the entire thing again. So while some of the circus people were setting up for that night's performance, the performers themselves got into costume and made an impromptu parade through the town. Calling attention to themselves, usually having a band, sometimes leading an exotic animal, when crowds gathered to see the spectacle of who was walking down their own Main Street the leader of the circus announced that evening's schedule and advised of what they would see if they came to the circus. Just a quarter to get in, a wealth of entertainment to be had, a deal that would be hard to pass up for so many. There were few sources of pure entertainment otherwise available, and people just had to provide themselves with whatever little asides they could get from some long, hard days of work. Because, no matter how I present the farm life it remains a serious lot of work that doesn't always end with any sort of success. What it does give to sort of replace "fun" is well-toned muscles, stamina, and a generally long life that ends up somehow being extremely productive. In spite of those times when a big wind took away a whole season's worth of harvest. Or crows decimated the corn yield, or a million other disappointments that destroyed all the work that had gone into one or more farm efforts. Which is why usually farm families were so big. It took a lot of little hands to help with some parts of the farming requirements. Families that had a lot of boys could keep it all going and looking perfect like some kind of fantasy. Families that had a lot of girls could do much the same but they would have to round up men and boys from the area to help during the busiest harvest. Which is often how marriages came to happen, just as a by-product of putting up hay or some such extremely physical work.

Anyway, on the day the circus was setting up across the road from their house, the boys went to see what was going on, and decided to put themselves into the action. They offered to work with the men setting up, in exchange for tickets to that night's show. They knew in their hearts that their mother would never fork over a quarter apiece to get in, so they traded an entire day of seriously hard labor for such a small amount as that. The last time my dad ever worked so hard for so little, as he learned his lesson well.

So during the whole day of helping out, they got to see the circus from a viewpoint most people never saw. At the end of the day they dragged their tired little selves back across the road and into their beds. Falling into deep sleep still wearing their clothes, they slept so soundly that they didn't hear the rest of the family go out. The ringmaster had come to their house that day asking permission to set up the circus on their property, and in return giving the whole family a free pass to get in that night.

What happened was that most of the family got in free to see the show, but the two who tried to get that for themselves were just too exhausted to go. Still, they'd seen something unique. People in regular clothes, not costumes, doing the same kind of physical work they saw their own father and uncles and older brothers doing most other days. But they would have liked to see the spectacle of performances that everyone would talk about for a long time to come.

RHEUMATIC FEVER

On his birthday in 1915 Clarence turned 9 years old. Because records were kept so randomly, he was thought to have been born in 1907 though it was later proven to have been 1906. So the year he was 9, when the whole family thought he was 8, he had started in 3rd grade at school.

Like most rural people, that school was a one room building donated by a local farmer. It was attended by all children who lived inside 2 miles from that building. There was only one employee, that was a very low-paid teacher who often lived as a guest in one of the farm homes of the area. Most often a young girl with nearly no income demands, such as would happen if the teacher were older, married, with children of their own, or other family member who depended on them for support. Some girls went straight from 8th grade graduation in May to being a teacher the following September. This school year revolved around the needs of the farm. All farm children had to help with planting and harvesting during that peak season, so school would be on vacation until the most of their work at home had been finished.

(Both my parents and all 4 of my grandparents went to this same kind of school. Walking to and from school, chores before and after school, sharing information at an incredible rate due to overhearing what subjects the older classes were being taught. Often the teacher was an unmarried girl or woman but at least one of those teachers was a man. Classically low wages were paid, teachers only able to teach what they had learned, the curriculum at least in farm country revolved around the 3 R's of Reading, Writing, and Rithmetic. Those subjects were given most of the school day, with additional subjects of penmanship and geography and a little bit of history. People of the pre-World War 1 years knew long poems which they could recite in front of a group. They had excellent cursive skills, and they all knew the first rule which was, "Neatness counts. If I can't read what you wrote I will give you an F for Fail." So homework was strictly handed in with the correct answers whenever possible, but primarily clean copy. There was to be no smear of anything, no remnant of words left over after erasing, and no holes in the paper due to zealous erasing, either. It was a strict routine that some people did well, others not so well, but the entire class stayed on topic until the last person in that class understood the lesson of that day. Either that or else stay at school until they did understand, maybe having to walk home in the dark, be in trouble with the parents, all manner of dire consequences. Thus, there wasn't the idea of nobody caring what homework they turned in, or paying attention to what the teacher was instructing. School was serious business to everybody. Parents chipped in money to pay the teacher and they would be looking for results because everybody was heavily invested in the matter of teaching children all that they would need for the grown up world, inside those 8 years of formal education. There were some people who went higher than 8th grade but I never heard of any farm child getting to do that. Once a decent education had been provided, that child was expected to pick up work and to take it in stride, sometimes moving from the family home at the same time. Other times the child would continue to live in the family home and contribute funds to the household especially if there were very old or very young family members to provide for, since really nobody made a lot of money from farming.)

So here it was, 1915. Clarence had lost his paternal grandfather the year before, and his paternal grandmother that same year. (These were Samuel Hacker b 1827 and Catherine Ann (Pottorff) Hacker) and this was before the Spanish flu and World War 1 found their way to Missouri.

One day probably in fall Clarence went home from school with a bad throat. He woke up with strep throat, and that disease had to run its course since pennecillin wasn't discovered until 1928.

One of the things strep throat could do to children was to turn into something else. If it took special hold in the brain it developed into St. Vitus Dance which is a nerve condition that causes its victims to jerk uncontrollably, though it is by no means a dance. (See some really old fairy tales about people dancing until they died, since this version of strep throat had been known for centuries. This condition was 100% fatal.

Alternatively, strep throat could settle in the heart. There were actually some survivors of this version, but because it always struck in childhood the body was suspended in its growth from the onset of the illness. Clarence was lucky in that his settled in his heart. A doctor was called to the house, in the times when all rural doctors made housecalls routinely, and the diagnosis was that he would soon die of it. This version is called Rheumatic Fever. Most of its victims died, but for those who recovered, their bodies were forever weakend. Many of the survivors didn't live to be very old as a result of damage done to them in those important growth years.

So, the doctor wasn't being an alarmist when he said death was imminent. His prescription was complete bed rest flat on his back, nothing to eat except clear broth, and to give him the best they could as far as attention and comfort. He was put to bed on the sofa in the parlour where he'd hardly been allowed to go before that time. It was a treat for him to look at all the nice furniture and the decorations in the parlour, which was his only entertainment what little time he was awake. He slept a lot, took clear broth several times a day in place of meals, and of course didn't go back to school.

His brothers and sisters came in to play with him when they got home from school. So there was a sharing of what they'd learned that day. But penmanship was out of the question. Sometimes they would read to him but he did very little reading for himself. Instead he had a raging fever and spent most of the time sleeping. It went on like that for 2 years until finally he was pronounced cured. The disease had run its course and left his heart enlarged. He would go through the whole rest of his life with heart issues. But, he survived in spite of poor health. From that time on he probably never again had a day like all his earlier days when he was so hearty and active. For all that he missed in school, he taught himself all he cared to learn. Because he never went back to school once he recovered. Basically he had the ability to read and write and do standard arithmetic. These were things all his siblings also had, but there were still those who didn't have as much formal education. At the same time there were in cities especially to the east some people went beyond 8th grade but for farm children across the agricultural regions they might get as much as 8th grade, or they might not. Most of what they had to learn came from working beside the rest of the family. Or, if their father had a skill he would teach it to them. Learning was very much up to the individual. Formal education was not valued for people who expected to earn a living on the farm. Because, at the end of all that, what could you do with that knowledge? That's the question. Instead of staying in school, many children went into the work force and my dad was one of them.

LEAVING HOME

After 2 years of complete bedrest and nothing to eat except for clear broth, Clarence finally recovered from his illness. I think the disease must have run its course but of course leaving organs damaged. Though he was in his growing years, rheumatic fever seems not to have stopped his growth. His father was a little shorter than he was but his brothers were about the same size as him. And he did continue to grow past the age of 10 or 11.

But the time came when he had to leave the comfort of living in the parlour surrounded by the nicest things the family owned. He went back to sleeping in the boys' bedroom and the parlour was then available for entertaining company. Such as his sister Janie's boyfriend and others who came to visit.

This was about the time when he realized his parents didn't get along. He remembered hearing them argue after all the children were supposed to be asleep. And he remembered that Grandpa and Grandma sometimes went in the evening to play cards with friends, and also to attend dances. The rest of his life he hated playing cards or any sort of gambling. He also hated dancing. These are the things he thought were responsible for his parents not getting along.

For whatever reason we can't know, those arguments grew into a divorce. So it was that by the time he was 13, my dad had to go out and make his own living. Because the family home was split and he couldn't stay with either of his parents or any other of the many relatives, he found a job as a farm worker on a nearby farm.

For his long days he was given a place to sleep in the hayloft of the barn and he took meals with the farmer's family. But nobody was nice to him. The farmer cussed him out continuously and no matter how hard he worked, was always grumbling for how costly it was to keep this poor little boy with nowhere else to go.

When I heard that story it made me hate that farmer. I cried for my sweet little daddy being treated like dirt, but he never cried as he told the story. Instead, he said that was the time when he decided he'd be his own boss so he didn't have to take anybody's cussing him out. And now I think, maybe that hard cruelty forced him to get strong from his long illness. Maybe without that awful farmer he wouldn't have lived a lot longer than 13 short years.

And then, the first chance he got, he found a better job. He left that original job to work for a prosperous dairy farmer, with a decent place to sleep, and nobody begrudged him what he ate. In fact, the new employers turned out to be a childless couple who treated him like the son they'd always wanted to have. Showing him how they wanted things done, he learned how to take care of a herd, which he hadn't done before that time. Beyond the milking and other duties of the dairy farm, he learned to drive a horse-drawn wagon to deliver milk to some of the customers. This kind of work freed the farmer to do other things, and the farm did well during that time. Clarence earned money though I don't know how much. Finally he had a situation he could count on, and free time to visit his brothers and sisters, his father, and his mother. He had time to spend in town, that was Gallatin which was the county seat and having its boom time just then, the 1920's.

MOTORCYCLE INCIDENT

During his early teens he kept close contact with his immediate family. He had other friends as well, knowing most of the local families since his earliest years. There were still lots of people he didn't know, even in Gallatin. That's the amazing thing about small towns. Everyone does their own routine of work and play. Those activities sometimes include the entire community but most often it is dealing with the same people day after day that determines who knows who.

This is the only way I can explain that there were in fact black people in Gallatin in those years while my dad was growing up. I never saw or even heard of black people as close to home as that. I had seen black people, of course, but those were all just people of the city as we drove along on our way to visit family. They were always just somebody else, not someone to have some reason to hate at all. And much later I learned through genealogy research that the ancestors weren't slave owners though they lived in some of the places where slavery was most prevalent. I think it's because we have always known, if you want a thing done right, you do it yourself. You do not in any case allow other people to do what's most important in your life. So slavery wouldn't have appealed to them as much as is to be known about them from court records, wills, and other documents. No slave was added into a will since possibly the early 1700's but there is a dispute over identities of the people involved. So I can't say no ancestor of mine ever owned a slave, but I can say I don't find any such indication in all the research I've done. Which is a thing I once worried about.

I have basically forgotten the story of my dad and his rowdy days involving one brother's motorcycle and another brother riding behind him. But the story survives because of you and your razor sharp memory.

If my dad was in his first job he would have been 13. His oldest brother Uncle Charle would have been working alongside their father on their farm. (This was the oldest farm son's expected inheritance and he would have been the one most involved in keeping that farm running. This is also the reason for military exemptions for that son not to be called up for World War 1. My Uncle Charlie did go into the navy in 1921 I believe, once the war was over. He served on the USS Enterprise and he went to the Pacific during his time in the navy. He scored high on marksmanship. I had a limited record of his military service because after the death of his wife Aunt Frances he left no direct descendants. As his brother's daughter, I am as close as it would be possible but still, they didn't send the entire account of his military service since I am not his child.)

I would think in 1918 or 1919 that Uncle Charlie would have been the brother who owned a motorcycle. It could have been Uncle Roy though, he was maybe 2 years older than my dad. But either way, he borrowed his brother's motorcycle. He knew how to get it started but forgot about how to stop it. His brother Uncle Walter was the one who went riding with him, and they got into a crowd on the square in Gallatin, and not knowing how to stop, ran right into an older woman who was black. She told them off so she must have been more scared than actually hurt in the incident. She called them White Trash but likely she said a whole lot more than that.

MILK DELIVERY JOB ROUTE/MEETING MY MOTHER

Throughout my childhood both my parents told stories of their lives. Each one separately or else the two of them in combination, the story always started with how they met. It was that pivotal moment in each of their lives, the time when the entire direction of the future changed. I can think of 3 pivotal moments in my own life but for them, it was just this one encounter that shaped the rest of their lives.

Upon leaving her family farm outside Maysville, MO, Maud Alta Parton took the trainride to Gallatin. Having borrowed the trainfare from her Grandma Parton (Sara (Sharp) Parton) she reached the big city later that same day. Walking the streets around the square, she looked in each shop window for the Help Wanted sign that was the biggest way businesses did their hiring in the 1920's. She would have been 19 but she believed she was 18 because birth records were so casually kept. So the year was 1925. The oldest girl in a family with 11 children would have been trained in keeping house and cooking for everyone and my mother started her training at the age of 6. She had to stand up on a stool to reach the dishes so that she could wash and dry them. Her father taught her to do that. Her mother was in poor health and spent most of her life bedridden as I understand it.

So Maud was extremely capable by that age, all the things a girl was required to know and even a little bit of reading, writing, and arithmetic. The jobs that would have been open to her on that day were clerk in a retail shop like her Grandma Parton did, or else cleaning other people's houses as many girls her age did, but the best opportunity she found was at the enormously popular Gallatin Hotel. It was popular because many people were getting into the habit of touring the country since cars were more often seen, and trains were still major transportation, and then still the horse drawn buggies that many people used. So travel really had its attraction for people of her generation. Women were able to vote. The devastating flu and world war were over. People were optimistic for that decade, and it was a great time to be just under 20 years old.

Mama had an interview on the spot with the hotel owner. He told her he would hire her for the kitchen, give her a room to share with another employee, and her meals. Wow! The most privacy she'd ever had in her life, only 1 other person to share a bedroom. And not paying rent or food costs, her $4 per week wage was entirely disposable income.

But, he warned her, "I know your father. If you can't be a good girl, I will tell him.

She thought of that a lot in the days ahead. "How does he know Poppy?" she asked herself repeatedly. But finally she understood, it was just him having warned her that she kept on being a good girl. This was, after all, the roaring 20's. Her roommate was That Old Helen Minnick, who had no intention of being a good girl, so there were choices that she made based on what she would never want her father to hear about her. To me, it was the idea of keeping order among the staff, more than any attempt to actually rule the lives of his employees. In any case, it all went smoothly in her job.

At first she washed dishes. Then she learned some of the cooking duties, and she had a day off every week. Wow! Another first for her hard working life. Money which she first sent back to Grandma Parton to repay her for the loan of that trainfare. Then she sent $2 out of every paycheck to her father to help him provide for the rest of the family. She was the only one of the 11 children who so far had left home. She even had a friend outside the family, That Old Helen Minnick who worked as a waitress in the dining room and was her roommate. She and her friend used a manual curling iron, just a long tubular thing made of iron like they would have used a different shape of iron to iron their clothes. Put it on a hot stove or else stick it into the fire to heat, then apply to hair or to clothing. Invariably there would be some singe or roast marks on the garment, but it just burned the hair if they used it too hot. They also backcombed their hair to make it look fuller. In my own teen years that was called "teasing" the hair, making it full of tangles and then just smoothing across the surface.

On her day off she and her friend Helen would walk around the square and buy things in the shops along the way. The first thing Maud bought for herself was a Kodak Brownie camera. It was just a small box and the film was purchased on a roll, to be put into the box carefully, then rolled to the first possible place to take a picture. If you forgot to forward the film once a picture was taken then you would get another picture over the top of the first one, next time you clicked the button to take a picture. Some very interesting double exposures were likely to come out of every roll but you wouldn't know that until you had your roll developed.

That little box camera would have cost as much as $2 if she bought it on one payday, or else more than that if she saved a couple of paychecks before purchase. It wasn't expensive at all, but buying the film and then paying for developing meant the hobby of photography was a bit of an expensive choice. That same camera worked without a bit of maintenance for the next 40 or more years. She was still taking excellent pictures with it in the 1960's. She only stopped using it when Kodak stopped selling the film that would fit, but the camera itself never stopped working. How much farther could you spread $2 or so? That would be about 50 cents per decade, not to mention capturing so many people and events as that camera did!

One of her first trips home to Maysville she took a picture of her whole family lined up in front of their one room house. Only her shadow shows that she was the one taking the picture. She had them all facing into the sunlight which is how she always posed people. Naturally, they weren't smiling as might have been in the case if they'd been in shade instead. But that is one of the few pictures ever taken of her brother Tommy. That's the brother who died at age 18 from a surgery to his mastoid, which was done at a hospital.

There was a day when Maud and That Old Helen Minnich were walking around the square, when a young man came toward them and passed them by. From behind them, he called out, "Hey you." They turned around. Helen had a stylish parasol that day, and she twirled it around behind her face as she smiled and said, "Who, me?" "No," he answered. "The little fat girl."

It was such a shock to both the girls, Maud turned around in a rage and walked away with her chin held high. Fat? What kind of thing was that for a stranger to say? She didn't look his way again but she heard him laughing loudly for a long time as she moved on down the street.

It was a few days later when she saw that same rude guy again. This time he was delivering milk to the kitchen while she was at work. She recognized him right away. It had been raining and he was thoroughly soaked. He complained how wet it was outside. So she said, "So what? You're not sugar nor salt nor nobody's honey!" That was her way of insulting him back for having called her fat.

"Oh no? I thought I was yours!" was his quick response. Then that same loud laugh as she blushed and turned back to her work

It doesn't seem like much but somehow those couple of odd meetings turned into 57 years of marriage. Clarence kept up that laughing but he had kind of been in love since the day he called her fat. She wouldn't go out with him for a long time but sooner or later he invited her to go to a movie one night. It turned out to be the silent version of Cecile B. DeMille's Ten Commandments which was showing at the Gallatin theater.

That really was quite a movie for its time. I saw it once, really did have a cast of thousands. It was the most professionally made movie I've ever seen out of the silent era but I haven't seen very many of them. Talkies wouldn't happen until they were married and had the oldest of their children. Though they didn't approve of movies in general so I don't think they ever again went to see a movie until the 1950's when old movies were played on television.

Many things happened during 1926 and 1927, they were split up for a time but then got back together. Of course it was That Old Helen Minnick who was behind the whole thing but fortunately for her she soon married her own young man and got out of being Maud's roommate.

The break up was kind of a funny story, with Helen seeing her young man for 4 years, yet he hadn't proposed to her. To speed that situation up a bit she told Clarence that Maud had a date with a married man. So he asked her to go out, and she gladly walked the square with him so that word would soon reach her young man. Sure enough, the next day he was so worried that she might marry someone else that he proposed to her, and That Old Helen Minnick was taken off the Singles list. But Maud wouldn't speak to Clarence for having gone out walking with her friend. Where everybody in town would see and talk about it. So they were split up for a time, which was very sad for Clarence. Maud declared she wouldn't have him if his head was strung with gold. Whatever that means. That's what she always said about it.

Uncle Roy changed her mind, though. What a talker he was! In the family he was always famous for the way he could talk. He would have been a good lawyer but instead, he just worked hard and kept that talking up for all his long life. I enjoyed his conversation. He was a funny person with strong opinions which he delivered in 25 words or less, without a hint of a smile. He did have eyes that betrayed laughter but otherwise no trace of humor escaped him.

This is as good a place as any to say a few things about the rest of my dad's siblings. I knew Uncle Charlie as an older man who looked the world and all like his own father, and my dad much younger, but I could see just how my dad would look in his later years. Uncle Roy more favored their mother and he always kept his hair, while the rest of the Hacker men were balding and then extremely bald. With beautiful eyes, every one of them. My dad had the most expressive eyes. It wasn't so much that his whole face moved with emotion, but I could read in his eyes what things he left unsaid. It's hard to explain, for anyone who never knew him. His siblings and his father had that way about them, but not to the extent that my dad had. I don't remember enough about my Grandma Hacker to say if she also had expressive eyes. I know she expressed herself in short, to the point, no misunderstanding kind of talk. It's what she was most known for in the family

I also knew Aunt Janie, my dad's favorite sister, and her husband Uncle John Laney. She was always very sweet to my dad. She played piano beautifully. She kept her looks well into old age, like their mother. And she lived to the age of 98. At the nursing home where she lived in her last years, she would go out for a walk right after breakfast, walk all around the grounds, and only come back for lunch. She was someone I admired and would like to be like but I can see already she has the record for oldest person in the family who walked half the day.

Uncle John Laney talked really slow. He was from South Missouri and always made us laugh with the things he said. Once we went to visit them at their home in Independence. Before we left home we called to get the address and directions to their house, then took the hour and a half or longer drive to Kansas City. As he told us, we were to look for Independent Blvd. and being a main street, we found it with no problem.

Uncle John had given us the address of one hundred and nineteen Independence Blvd. We looked for house numbers, found our way into the lower numbers along that road, but there was no 119 though we went up and down that street several times looking for it. Finally we pulled over and called them again. I was the one who talked to Uncle John, told him we couldn't find 119 Independence Blvd. and asked for further directions. That's when he told it all out, not the

119 that I had written down when he said one hundred and nineteen, but the number was actually 10019. That's right. One hundred. And 19. After that, it was a short drive to the right address, and I've always remembered how we laughed over that misunderstanding. Anyway we had lunch with them, sat in the living room while Aunt Janie played us some songs, and then we went home.

While we were there she kept looking at her feet. Even while keeping up conversation, she would be looking at different angles of her feet. All that family were proud of having little bitty feet but Aunt Janie was the proudest of them all.

I also knew Aunt Nora and her husband Uncle Carl Fulton. She had the same face as their mother and she also kept her looks into old age. When she got married she and Uncle Carl moved to one of the north suburbs of Kansas City. She worked outside the home, which was fairly common by the time of World War 2 but not so much when she was doing it in the 1930's. Uncle Carl was a union steward at the Ford plant (north of Kansas City maybe it was GlenLake or some such town, Glendale, you know something like that) and the two of them were staunch Democrats. Many arguments happened between them and my dad because they couldn't discuss politics at all. My dad was a staunch Republican, very supportive of Ike, President Dwight D. Eisenhower who happened to look a lot like the Hacker men, just by the way.

So those were the 4 siblings of my dad who were still living by the time I was a child. I didn't know Aunt Marjorie, or Uncle Walter, or Aunt Bessie, or Aunt Maggie. Those 4 siblings had passed away before I was born. But for my Hacker grandparents, how sorry I felt for their having lost 4 children in their lifetime! Their other 5 children all lived into old age.

FIRST CAR

When Daddy was little of course, most people went around on horseback or else in horse-drawn buggies, or else on foot. He didn't remember the covered wagon trips but he was part of that episode of American history. But because his Uncle Dan had a car business he was somewhat familiar with cars.

The first thing he bought for himself when he started working for wages, was a pair of long work gloves. He had his picture taken where he was showing off his fine new work gloves that came nearly halfway to his elbows. This was what he needed during harvest and he took pride in those gloves. But one thing besides that he bought for himself when he'd saved up $25 was a used car. So $25 might be roughly equal to 3 months' savings. Anyway, a neighbor man had a Model T that he wanted to get rid of, my dad went to his house, looked it over, paid the $25 asking price, and drove it away. That was all. No driver's license. No license plates. Just start it up and put it into gear and go.

It was because of that first car that he was always careful to let me know that I had no business telling him how to drive. I felt like I needed to have that serious talk with him when he lived in Belton, on the way home driving on the big highway of all things, and he missed his turnoff. So, to compensate for that, he just backed up until he could take that exit. On a busy highway, of all things! I was terrified for both my parents when I found that out. Yet, I didn't have the guts to tell my dad he should stop driving. Instead, I just said I will be happy to take you anywhere you want to go. So let me know, will you do that? Oh, of course if I need a ride I will. But I don't need a ride since I have a car. I needn't to tell you that I was still a little bit scared of my dad even in my 30's when he was in his 70's! It was just lucky for all of us that he let his driver's license lapse and then couldn't get it renewed due to his bad heart and all the doctor evidence that was on record!

MARRIAGE AND FAMILY; HOW MY PARENTS MET

Maud Alta Parton was born 22 September 1906 on a farm 2 miles outside of Maysville, MO in Dekalb County. To the east of town.

Lots of her Parton relatives lived near but the one she visited most often was her Grandma Parton, Sara (Sharp) Parton. This lady had a house and garden in Maysville. She walked a few blocks to a drug store where she worked. Maybe she was a cashier, or possibly a clerk in the office. That was never fully explained to me. But she also had rooms to rent in her house, kept her garden to supplement the family's needs, and sometimes did laundry for other people. To me, that's a strong woman doing what it took to raise her children and some of her grandchildren. She was married to Henry Parton but he lived somewhere else so that she was basically a single mother and grandmother for many years.

During her lifetime in northwest Missouri and elsewhere in this country, it was a matter of shame for a woman to work outside the home. People didn't like to see women in a place of business unless she were just there to shop. There was a prejudice against women being seen anywhere in public. In family gatherings and church it was ok for women to go among people, but escorted by a husband. There was also a prejudice against a man who would demean his wife so badly that she was forced to work outside the home. As though her husband couldn't provide. Yet, Sara did what needed to get done. For that, I give her a big round of applause

I would never have guessed she had such a social obstacle to deal with day in and day out! It was only in biographies of women of that century that I came across such detail as that. It seems odd in this century but must have seemed ordinary in her own lifetime since it was never mentioned at all. And people only ever tell things that were out of the ordinary because that's just human nature.

Among her other huge family members Maud knew some of her cousins, Uncle Charlie's children. She said those kids had a dog's life but that every one of them could make music out of thin air. Whether singing, beating rocks and sticks like a drum, or making a blade of grass do violin sounds, she said all those kids had the music in them. She had the music in her, too. My mother's singing voice was a high, clear, strong soprano and she always sang the lead. I just took harmony to back her up but really, my voice is lower so that alto is the one I can sing without straining. Mama could always carry a tune. She never lost that ability.

She had other cousins, aunts, and uncles that she saw less often. I think they must have lived beyond DeKalb county. She was often taken to her Grandma Parton's house. I think those times would have been while her mother was giving birth to the next sibling, since childbirth always happened in the home. For people in remote areas a doctor was sometimes available to them, and would make house calls. But for most physical needs they took care of those things themselves. Or else had the help of some of the women in the family. I never heard of any of them using a midwife or even that they knew someone who did that kind of work. Instead, it was each woman's multi-tasking routine to take care of all the family needs which sometimes included first aid and minor doctoring. For really serious things of course, they could get to somebody who had a doctor's license though those people weren't widely trusted in the family.

After Maud lived at the Gallatin Hotel and had her own money, she and her older brother Uncle Clarence went in search of their Fales grandparents. They'd never met their mother's parents though one of her brothers, Uncle Frank Fales used to visit them when all the children were small. So Maud and her brother Clarence took the train and went some distance, though she could never say where that was. They asked first one person and then another, until finally they arrived at the right train stop. Someone was there, with a horse and buggy. They asked him if he knew their grandfather, Francis Fales. He did. He said their grandfather was a prince of a man.

Mama always remembered how that made her feel, hearing such high praise of her unknown grandfather. And then that man drove them to the Fales home. It was after dark when they arrived. It was rare that anyone would be visiting at night but they knocked, the grandfather asked Who is it? And they answered they were Nellie's children, and so he let them come in. That was how they met Francis Fales and his wife Laura (Raymond) Fales. There was a long estrangement between them and their daughter, that's the only thing I ever knew about that. It seems my entire family has excelled at feuding, and that we always do the shun. Not a blood feud, at least. The shun is where you just don't have any contact with, or interaction between, members of the family. I happen to have learned the way to feud during my preschool years when two of my sisters became estranged from each other. So there is a history of that sort of thing going back for at least 100 years. Mama was never any good at feuding. She was the one who tried to get people to patch up their differences. She had various successes with that, but also many failures. Hard headed people, that's all I can say.

She didn't get that feud resolved but she did get to meet and speak with those grandparents. And then spend the night at their house before going home. In this way she came to know another cousin, that was Valentina Fales, daughter of Uncle Frank Fales. Valentina never married. She used to come visit us when I was a child, and she and Mama had a warm friendship.

BACK TO MY PARENTS' MARRIAGE

Once all their issues were resolved, Clarence Olin Dean Hacker and Maud Alta Parton were married. The date was February 14, 1928. Valentine's Day. Nobody since that year has been married on Valentine's Day though I think it would be a good day for a wedding.

That year it was blizzard weather, pretty typical for that area in any winter month. Aunt Nora had tried to talk my mom out of it. She said, "You shouldn't marry him. He won't live very long." but Mama knew her own mind and wouldn't be changing her mind very often just as a matter of honor. In fact in all the time I knew her, only once did someone change her mind, and that was Daddy's brother, Uncle Roy. Daddy's sister Aunt Nora didn't have his gift of words. All she had was her bossiness and most times that was all it took for her to get her point across. Not that time, though.

So, Gallatin, Missouri. The night before the wedding, they stayed with Aunt Janie and Uncle John. Girls in one bedroom, boys in another, as was to be expected. Early the next day they 4 all went to the Methodist minister's home. The parsonage next door to the Methodist church. They were married at his house, not in the church next door. No guests came to the wedding, just the 2 witnesses who stood up with them. The minister's wife played the piano and Mama got to walk down the aisle. After the ceremony, they moved right into the little house in the country where they were to live. And remember, it was only 8 months before the whole bottom of the economy dropped out from under the country. So soon after they married there was a lengthy depression, the groom with a bad heart, and by October, there was a child on the way. If you were to plan a worse start for any marriage, you could hardly imagine one worse than that! Still, there is something to be said about enduring tough times, how strengthening that can be to personal lives as well as to relationships, in certain instances. This marriage was one of those instances. In fact, it only ended when Clarence passed away 57 years later. Maud was a widow for the last 11 years of her life.

Getting through the Great Depression, health issues, and the draft,
Because the dairy had to lay him off, my dad had to look for other work. This was never a problem for him but his heart continued to dictate how much he could actually do. But here is the amazing thing. He could work and work, circles around people much younger than himself. He started early and stopped late, because he worked the job, not the hour. You would never guess him to be in poor health during such times. Yet, when his face turned sickly white and he got all sweaty hot and sat down, that was the time for alarm. It turns out that he'd had a series of heart attacks because in his later years having a pacemaker put in, they found lots of scar tissue in his heart.

Yet, he worked at first one thing then another, every day but Sunday. He did whatever came to his hand to do, except for things that were shady or even questionable. He had a standard for his behavior and I never knew him to lower his expectations of himself. Not for any sort of advantage would he compromise his work or his integrity or his honesty.

That's something to impress even a rebellious kid like I was, when I first noticed my dad wasn't doing things like all the rest of the people we knew.

For example, if he set out to harvest a field, he let nothing prevent his finishing that task. Not rain, not broken equipment, nothing got in the way of that work. It was his early training in how to raise crops and livestock, how he saw the direct connection to being able to provide for all the people as well as all the animals in his care, and so he worked hard and long to make it happen. Sometimes he did have help. People of that area have been known to help each other out in a reciprocal kind of way, or else for some small reward. My mother's brothers would help Daddy in harvest time just to get Mama's field hand dinner. Biscuits and gravy, fried chicken, fried potatoes, fresh vegetables out of the garden, and pies and cakes. She put together the same kind of meals as her brothers remembered from their childhood, and that was all the payment they could want. So lots of uncles came during harvest time.

Another source of income during the depression was that people's cars would drop off pieces as they drove some of those rugged dirt roads. Nothing makes deeper ruts than somebody going through it while it's mud. Anyway, he noticed metal laying beside the road, and so he would stop and pick that up. He had a pick up truck parked beside the house, and he kept throwing metal into it until it got full. Then he would drive that truck to St. Joseph where some Jewish brothers ran a junk yard, and they paid for metal by the pound. Those guys were also very impressed by my dad. They took the time to show him how to keep his records, which is the only accounting lesson he ever had, but which method he always used from that time on. For his part, he admired those brothers for their integrity and for their kindness to him.

I don't know if during the 1930's my parents had any idea what was going on in Europe. They had plenty to keep their attention focused right at their own home and it doesn't seem to me that there was a lot of world news getting all the way to them. After all, half a world away, a bunch of strangers, I can see why that wouldn't get a lot of attention when there were so many chores waiting to be done

Eventually they did find it all out, though. My oldest sister was 12 years old when Pearl Harbor was bombed on December 7, 1941. Some of the older cousins, and some of the younger of our uncles went off to that war. It came as quite a shock to them, having lived through World War 1 which was supposed to have ended all wars. Now suddenly World War 2 was happening and it even involved the farm lands and rural populations of Missouri and all the other Bread Basket states.

So it was hardly a surprise when a draft notice came for my dad. He was ordered to appear at an army base on a certain day, which he did. He didn't pass his exam though, and was rejected for service. At that time he was in his mid 30's, so the draft applied to a wider age group than I expected. He had a wife, 3 girls, and 1 boy at that time. He worked on a farm that belonged to someone else. In exchange for living in that house he put in some labor on the farmer's land, kind of like a feudal system the ancestors would have known some centuries before. But in addition to the house where they lived, they also had a little kitchen garden, a goat for milk since one of the children had lactose intolerance, a flock of chickens for eggs and meat, and tried every way to supply their own needs.

So that actual money hardly crossed their paths, yet all their needs were met, they practiced an extreme form of recycle and repurpose of the things they couldn't make for themselves. They had always known how to get through hard times, with only the few years in the 20's when money was easier to earn. So their training had prepared them for that long depression, and they even learned some good lessons during those years.

Such as logging. Walnut logs in particular, to identify the best of standing timber, to cut them down and get them to the mill with no loss of life, which is still a hard thing to do. My dad worked sometimes with crews who were cutting trees. This is how he learned all that he knew about walnut logs. Black walnut, I should say. You can know this tree by its bark which looks like the outside rind of a muskmelon. No other tree has that kind of bark. Anyway, over many years of experience, that became my dad's main source of income. Though never entirely dependent on that one source. My dad always had a litter of hogs that he could take to market any time he needed a quick few hundred dollars. And there was always more hay in the barn than his cattle could eat, so some of that could safely be sold. Plus his cows were dairy, not beef cattle, and he knew how the dairy worked. So he sold milk in the mornings, every day of the world while the cows were giving milk, and then he took a few months off from that while the cows went dry as they call it, when their calves were past the nursing age. In time each cow could be pregnant again, at which time the milk would flow. But even they need a time off to renew their strength!

GETTIING THROUGH WORLD WAR 2

During that war several of my cousins and uncles served in the army and in the navy. I know more about the cousins so here is the information I have;

Harold Vandiver, son of Aunt Janie and her first husband. He is the oldest of my Hacker cousins. He was a pilot during the war but was shot down. As a result of that he had injuries that prevented him from ever again flying. Because pilots have to be in perfect health this was an unavoidable detour in his life. He lived most of the rest of his long life working for NASA. He still knew all the pilot methods, though he couldn't do them any more. Still, his knowledge was used to train future astronauts. He was working at Houston on that night when we watched Neil Armstrong take his first steps on the moon, his son also went to work for NASA.

Marvin Fulton, son of Aunt Nora and Uncle Carl. He served in the navy and was involved in a battle at sea. While shooting at the enemy he noticed he wasn't pulling the trigger on his gun. When he looked at his hand he saw some of his fingers had been blown off, and that was the first he knew of it. He was discharged and went straight back to Missouri, married his high school girlfriend, and lived the rest of his life as a farmer.

Richard Fulton, another son of Aunt Nora and Uncle Carl. He asked his parents to come walk the field with him, and it was on that walk that he told them he was volunteering for the army. He told them his decision was made and asked them to respect that decision. This is the cousin who went into the CIA. He had something to do with the Bay of Pigs but that's all I know of it. Of course I know the world was almost blown up during that time. I just don't know what Richard had to do with it. Because of his life work, he retired but always lived right outside Washington, DC. He married a German girl, they had no children, and he is buried at Arlington Cemetery.

Uncle Jim Watkins, first husband of my Aunt Adelina, Mama's youngest sister. This uncle went to the army and served in Europe. I never heard him tell any of his war stories. He worked in logging during the 1950's. He died while his children were young. My aunt was devastated. She remarried some time later but nothing was ever the same for any of them.

Uncle Charlie had served in the navy right after World War 1. He married Aunt Frances Watson but they had no children. Uncle Charlie became a Nazarene minister at some point.

Most of my dad's generation were too young for World War 1 and too old for World War 2. But Daddy was instructed to go somewhere to test for the draft. He didn't pass his exam because as already explained, he had multiple health problems stemming from a bad heart. He was rejected from the draft and went back home where everyone was glad to have him back.

THE FARM OUTSIDE ALTAMONT AND THE ROAD TO WEATHERBY

Grandma and Grandpa Parton lived on a farm east of Altamont. It was down a muddy back road, left turn off Hwy 69, then right turn down that dirt road. That was a lovely drive. I sat in the front seat as Mama drove. I always sat in the front seat because I often got car sick riding in the back seat. And as we drove along with the windows down, it felt so nice to have the wind on our skin, surrounded by lush hedgerows and wild flowers that bordered all the fields along the way. Usually we saw Grandpa out plowing with his horse pulling the plow, himself walking behind. Mama would honk the horn and wave to him but he stayed at his work while we went on to the house.

My father used a tractor for his field work, so Grandpa was doing the much older version of that work. This is the grandfather who witched for water. I think I've explained that to you. And that is definitely a much older way of doing things! He was good with plants and animals, he kept bees, and he used the Old Farmer's Almanac to read the signs of the days. When the sign was in the head, he would plant tall things like corn. When the sign was in the feet, that was the time he planted root crops like potatoes, carrots, and turnips. His gardens and his fields always produced well so he could have been right about planting in the signs. Mama believed he was the ultimate expert on any farm question she might have. Daddy said it was a bunch of hooey. I didn't get involved at the time but I have had a few laughs over those disagreements. My parents were hilarious whenever they disagreed. But that wasn't very often because most of the time they were side by side and in agreement on everything.

One more thing I've just remembered about Grandpa Parton. Because today is the 3rd Thursday in November, I am reminded that this was the day he always said was the REAL Thanksgiving. The date had been changed to the last Thursday in November but he never failed to bring that up. Still, for the sake of getting along, he celebrated Thanksgiving with the rest of the family. When we all lived on farms of course, Thanksgiving meant something like a harvest festival. It was directly tied to that year's harvest so we celebrated another year of having done so much work. As such, there was no Black Friday shopping and bargain hunting. Places were open over the 4 day weekend, and of course no farmer gets a day off, but really it was all about having been successful in our attempt to feed ourselves and our animals and then put our land to bed for the winter. We had enough food to get through winter with canned vegetables, fruits made into jams, and a certain amount of smoked meats. Mostly Daddy hunted for meat in winter. Or else we could butcher an animal and then share it with family since it wouldn't be possible to smoke a whole calf or anything.

During my childhood every small town in the area had a business they called the locker. It was a freezer building where you could rent different sized boxes and store your frozen food. Then people would go to their locker and get out enough meat and other items to last for a while, and this cost about $2 per month. Which was above the minimum wage when I had my first job. Still, it was one of the choices people could have for winter storage if canning and smoking and fresh butchering didn't cover everything. But when I was in high school Mama and Daddy bought their own chest freezer and it was set up in my bedroom. Again, right off the kitchen. So once they had that of course, could handle a whole hog and half a beef with plenty of room for frozen vegetables. But it was probably about 10 years before town lockers went out of business due to so many people owning their own freezers.

Before those times, farmers lived on what produce they planted, including grains along with fruits and vegetables. These could be stored as generations before them, by drying the grains then keeping in a crock or heavy container to prevent bugs and mice from getting into the food. Long many hours of boiling jars then filling with vegetables before stacking them on long shelves. Hot and tiring work that was! But the food supply had to last until spring when asparagus and mushrooms might spring up volunteer in the weeks before peas and radishes and leafy greens could be planted. Fruits were made into jams for keeping through the winter. I remember hot biscuits spread with homemade butter and jam, since there wasn't always time for gravy to be made. Such as on laundry day. We were otherwise occupied and spent little time in the kitchen those busy days.

But farmers also had to provide the long months of food for all their animals. So twice in summer we all go into the fields when the alfalfa was ready to be gathered into hay. Daddy estimated generously how much feed his animals would need to get through the winter. Once spring was back, new calves being born, all the cattle grazed in the pastures around the pond. There they had easy access to get a drink as often as they wanted. So in summer, whatever he portioned for his animals would be from the first mowing. That hay was kept out in the field in big rectangle shapes, then loaded onto a flatbed and pulled to the barn. Then each bale was hoisted with ropes and pulleys to stack in the second floor of the barn. When that much was done, all the rest of the hay bales from that mowing and the second mowing, were taken to the sale barn. That was a business with an auctioneer, farmers went there on Wednesdays to bid on hay, seed corn, animals, and sometimes machinery for their farm needs. So this was a place where Daddy sold his excess hay. It was one of the year's paydays for him.

With so much attention paid to the land and the animals on it, you may well imagine how happy Thanksgiving was for us. We always had Thanksgiving at Grandma and Grandpa Parton's house with all Mama's siblings and their families. There the women would gather around the wood burning kitchen stove to bake and roast all the traditional foods. We also brought lots of prepared food from home, things that could be served without further cooking, like cakes and pies and jars of pickles and such as that. It was a day to laugh and play with the cousins, to see the men sitting around talking, and to run errands for any of the women who needed something from the root cellar. Thankful for the food of that day of course, but equally thankful so much work was finally finished.

We didn't spend every minute working, I need to clarify that. Work was unavoidable and usually done by lots of people. But there were times when I had to do my chores without help. Work was all around us. Yet demands on our time was more in some seasons, less in others. Winter was when the land rested and so did we. Even so, animals still needed food and water and were especially susceptible to predators. This is why everybody on the farm knew how to shoot. We cared for the animals in all the ways they couldn't care for themselves, and farm animals have long lost their ability to defend themselves from predators.

I was taught to shoot tin cans off the fence. Later I got to go squirrel hunting with Daddy and a friend of his, who also brought his son. That was the only time I was allowed to hunt. Good thing it was, too because those squirrels soon taught me they already knew a few things about self defense. They could run so fast, I could barely keep them in sight. And they ran in spirals around the tree trunks until they tucked back into their homes up high where they were well hidden in all the leaves. That's all the shooting I did but we all knew how to do that if necessary. There were wolves and foxes in the area. There were weasels, too, so we tried first of all to keep those things from getting in the barn or the hen house. The field corn was stored in a sort of separate container called a silo, and sometimes predators would try to get into that, too. But for the most part, Daddy and the rest of the men hunted raccoons. Daddy had some very expensive coon hounds that were only for his hunting. We weren't allowed to play with them at all. Mama raised cocker spaniels to sell to pet stores, and those we did get to play with. It was so sad when she sold each one, except for Honey which was a blonde cocker with deformed front legs who never could run very well. That one we kept and he was babied so much. So we had dogs, and sometimes cats who lived in the barn, when Grandpa had so many kittens he had to give some away. So animals were always part of the farm. Only the hogs were off limits to me. I could feed them from the fence but Daddy was the only one who could go in among them. They can't be trusted and really, are still not domesticated in the way that cattle are. We didn't have horses or goats or sheep so I know much less about them than I do about cows and chickens. For personality reasons I liked certain cows better than others, but all the chickens were sweet little things.

There were some children chores and these were even done by older children without any complaint. For hand-powered equipment little hands could do it as well as bigger ones, and it sort of included everybody because it was something we could all enjoy once finished. One of my earliest memories is of turning the crank to churn the cream into butter. It took so long, got one arm so tired, then I had to switch to the other arm, and still that cream wasn't a solid! It was most annoying. But then Mama had my brother take a turn while I had time to play. Then it was my turn again, and after nearly forever, Mama finished the whole thing off and turned the butter out onto a plate. This wasn't done every day because we didn't use it all up so fast as that. But any additional cream that came in from the day's milking could also be made into ice cream. In the long hot summer days it was a really nice thing to have! We made it after our supper and enjoyed it in the last bit of daylight, sitting outside in the cool of the day. That was much like the churn, or at least was made by the same killing use of the hand and arm to turn the crank until the liquid inside the canister was too solid for the blades of the ice cream freezer to go any further. That's how we knew it was finished.

THE OLD GAS STATION ON HIGHWAY 6 AND WHAT BECAME OF THAT PROPERTY

I can just barely remember living somewhere else. I don't know where that house was. But one day we went somewhere in the car, to a little closed up gas station on a road sitting there all by itself, with some trees close by. I can't remember ever going back to the house we'd been living in but soon we moved into that gas station. It was 3 rooms, and lots of uncles and Grandpa Parton kept coming there and doing a lot of outside work. I was kept inside most of that time. But in a while there was a new house, and we moved into it. I remember the strong smell of wood in the new house. It was a pleasant house. I had the yellow bedroom off the kitchen. And that is the house where the rest of my childhood was spent.

When I was high school Daddy heard something about the plans for a big highway to come somewhere near. It was supposed to connect Des Moines, IA all the way to Kansas City, MO. Such a thing was exciting to think about. We lived between those two cities and it took a long time to drive to either one. But if a big highway connected them, we would be able to go to one city in 2 hours or less! No turning down back roads and crossing dangerous bridges like the one at Pattonsburg that kept flooding out and causing accidents. Until that time we had to rely mostly on old Highway 69 for our north to south travel, and old Highway 36 for our east to west trips. We were all interested in the idea and occasionally we heard more about it. Somebody the folks knew sold part of their farm to the highway once it got to the north side of Bethany.

But I was grown up and moved to Waukegan and had 2 children before the end of that story. It was a delight to me, on one of our trips to visit the family. I was able to drive from Waukegan, IL on Highway 41 then take the hateful tollroad around Chicago, before connecting to Interstate 80 at Joliet and Romeoville. That part of the trip took so long because there was constant construction and lane closures that toll road and in years to come I found a solution to going the Chicago way. But 80 all the way to Des Moines was a wonderful separated 4 lane highway and I easily found the connection to Interstate 35 from there. We drove south to Bethany, where construction stopped. Good thing for me I knew little Highway 13

And as the highway continued, so too did people come to talk to Daddy about a little corner off his property, just at the east. They weren't entirely settled on the final path the road would be built but surveyors were out in the area looking for the workable solution to that last piece of I-35 to be completed. One thing Daddy learned from talking with neighbors, if a farmer named his price and that figure was exorbitant, the highway would just divert elsewhere. If a farmer named a low price thinking it was negotiable, the highway would give only the amount he first named, and either take it or leave it. So, with the highway having all the advantage in such a negotiation, Daddy chose not to name his price at all. Instead, he kept asking, "How much were you expecting to spend?" until they named the figure, and that is the one he accepted. No negotiations happened at all, which was a big shock to everyone in that area.

And what ended up, because of the highway taking a corner off the east, they actually bought the whole place but gave back all that they didn't need to build the cloverleaf and put the last section of that highway in place. So, that abandoned gas station on 40 acres, where sat that little green house on the south side of old Highway 6, that Daddy bought on a $4000 note from the bank and paid on for 10 years, basically paid him all those years of living expenses. The house and grounds were owned outright. Every year several days of income came from the land, even when Daddy quit working the walnut logs still making a living on that property. And he was given $80,000 for the land, and got his house and grounds back anyway, all except for that eastern corner! So that's what became of that 20 or so years on that place.

After they received their money, they rented out that house and bought a house in Gallatin. The people who rented the green house outside of Winston had a fire, and being so far from help, the house and garage both burned to the ground. After that, the folks bought a modular and had it set up on top of the hill on the north side of old Highway 6. The old barn was on that side of the highway, so when they moved back to the farm, they hadn't lost the ability to make a living on the farm. Plus, they each found out they were born in 1906 instead of 1907 as they'd always believed, and so were able to get social security coming in a year earlier than they expected. I never saw anyone be so happy to find out they were actually older than they thought!

Later, they sold that farm and moved to a house in Altamont. Then they sold that house and went to spend some time in Phoenix in Wava's neighborhood. Not in her house but in a house walking distance from her. Neither of my parents would consent to live in her house but they were able to spend some quality time with her at the end of their lives. They had been estranged from her for much of her life. It did very much affect Mama and Daddy but that being their child, they were eager to smooth things over and at least get to see her in their old age. They just let the past alone and were grateful that she had time for them by that time. I believe I have told you about the collapse of all civilization as we know it that happened when Max decided to divorce Earl, even though Wava decided she wouldn't. It came to an end a couple of decades later but left its mark on Mama and Daddy.

THE WINSTON COAL MINE

When I was in first grade playing outside at recess, I could clearly see the little triangle hill that marked the Winston coal mine. It hadn't been worked for a long time but still sometimes a fire would start there and we would see smoke coming out of it. Then volunteer fire department members would hurry over there and put it out.

When I was in 8th grade Daddy bought that coal mine and about ½ acre of ground that it sat on.

He used it as a place to put used cars that he would sell. More of a used car storage lot than anything else. We believed that the entire property was full of tunnels from the time when it used to be a working coal mine. So there was never a plan to build on it because we feared the land wasn't stable enough to support a building. I never could understand why he would want such a piece of land but it could be he had ideas for it that he just didn't share with me. I don't know what became of the whole thing because by the time the folks moved to Gallatin that coal mine was no longer one of his properties.

THE GHOUL FAMILY FARM
AND THE JESSE JAMES BRIDGE

Since I was taking secretarial classes in school, I started writing Daddy's business letters. He would tell me what he wanted to say, I would come up with the verbiage, and then he would sign it. One letter I wrote was an inquiry about buying a farm east of Winston. It was 80 acres with a lot of excellent standing walnut trees, a house, a barn, and outbuildings. No one had lived there for some years. The family wrote back that they were interested in hearing his offer, and he made his own arrangements for meeting someone who could make a decision on that sale. It turned out that he was able to get the property. That one I know he intended to take out the best of the walnut, sell those logs at the saw mill, and make back the purchase price that way. But before that all happened, Paul got married and moved into that house. After some years, Daddy sold the whole property and never did get that timber out. He broke his leg during that time so it was the end of his logging business.

What he did after that time was to be a consultant for a big logging company. There he made more money than he'd ever made by cutting and hauling logs to the mill. He even said he wished he could have found that job years earlier. But soon or late, he was glad to end his career doing such easy work. He went to locations, checked the standing trees, estimated how much lumber would be involved, and submit his findings to the company. I don't know the name of that company, I was living in Waukegan at that time.

But that property, the one I wrote the letter of inquiry, was the property where the Jesse James gang had hid their horses under the bridge, while robbing the train. If someone had been sitting on the front porch of that house they would have been able to see the whole thing unfold.

So to sum up my dad's career, his many income methods, and his business ideals, these are some of the things he did.

Age 13 farm worker, lived in the barn, had his meals in the family kitchen, and worked from sunup to sundown for the farmer. That farmer cussed him out continuously and reminded him of the expense of his housing and his meals, this right after his recovery from rheumatic fever. He had no down time but he did cry in his bed at night, for all his rough treatment and for how much he missed his mother and all his family. Still, that farmer's rough treatment of him may have put him into better health just because it was so physically demanding.

As soon as possible he found another job at the dairy farm. There he slept in a room in the house and took his meals with the farmer and his wife. They were a childless couple who treated him like the son they'd never had. That farmer generously showed him all the jobs he could do on the farm. Plus when he learned the dairy work, then he was given the horse and cart delivery service as well, and had money to spend as he pleased. That job he kept for several years. The farmer and his wife remained his friends the rest of their lives.

He found a situation on a farm, one that included a house and grounds for his own use. In return for his living there he would help the farmer at busy times but this was not so often that he couldn't get another job. This is what he did once he married my mother. They lived in a house on the big farm, kept their own chickens and made a garden mostly mama's doing. In this way they provided food for themselves. There wasn't extra eggs or produce to sell but sometimes they had enough for their own use plus some to give to various family members. Meantime Daddy worked through the depression, doing whatever he could find to do for what little pay he could find. He said $1 a day was a good wage and some days of the month he made that much. Other days he made less, or else nothing. But the house and groceries were supplied by the days when he helped on the farmer's crops. Planting time would have been a little work. Weeding and watering would have taken part of some days. Only harvest would have been days on end, when no other job could be considered just because the time was completely taken for harvest.

Other depression work he did, a door to door pepper salesman. He was to ask someone to smell the pepper, and if that made them sneeze then he had to give them $1. The pepper was guaranteed not to make people sneeze so he sometimes made sales. He could earn $1 a day when he did that job.

He picked up metal he saw laying alongside the road. People might lose a muffler or a fender or any sort of part if they drove crazy fast over those mud ruts. This metal he put in his car and took it home. Then he put the metal into the pickup bed, and just left it there. Once there was a full load, he drove it to St. Joseph to the junk yard where they bought scrap metal so much per pound. This occasional income was entirely extra money, and the family was growing, so the money found a use. But it wasn't often that he had a load of scrap metal to sell.

He worked by the day on any of the local farms when there was a special need. For his labor he would get his lunch, and then some kind of pay at the end of the day. Maybe it would be in cash, or more likely it would be chickens that he could take home to use for eggs or meat.

One of the day jobs he found was helping cut down walnut logs. He learned to notch the tree in a very particular way, then go around to the other side of the tree and cut through to that notch. In that way he could decide exactly where he wanted the tree to fall. That was important because sometimes there were people or houses near where trees were being cut. But even out in the woods far from people, it was still good to lay that tree where it could best fall.

Sometimes it would happen that a tree would be cut down and only then was it known that there was a bee hive in its top branches. This is how he learned that he was allergic to bee stings. The only solution for it was to throw water on the bees. In that part of Missouri you are never far from a stream of some size, and getting the bees wet caused them to lose all their fight. Then all the men would rob the hive and take as much honey as they could put into pillowsacks. Always strong smelling and extremely dark, those honeycombs would be squeezed inside the pillowsacks and the honey would come out the other side of the fabric. This of course didn't happen in the woods, but when he brought those home. Mama is the one who did the processing of the honey since there might be dead bees in all that stuff, and their stingers might still scratch the skin. She wasn't allergic to bee sting so she could do that part without problems. That honey was always put to use instead of being sold. But if they bought honey in the grocery store that was one of the expensive items, so they only had honey when Daddy hit a bee tree.

Daddy learned to keep his own books, as he was taught by the men who owned that junkyard. He was very impressed with their integrity. He imitated them in his dealings with people, and the fact that they were Jews in the 1930's while World War 2 was about to start, those men would certainly have known what was happening to their relatives in Europe. I don't think my parents knew it though. They barely noticed what things were in the news, not having any news source except for what people said to each other. But many years later, my dad showed Paul's wife Jane how to keep Paul's books. She said he told it to her so clearly that she understood right away, and never forgot it.

I do want to describe the walnut log work because that was really the main income we lived on for my entire childhood. I had many experiences in the woods. It was a familiar kind of place to me though each visit to the woods had new things to see. In the woods behind the house on Highway 6 where the quick mud was, there were some arrowheads which I found just by pulling my shoes up out of the mud. I liked to think there may have been some settlements of Indian tribes at that spot, and that could have been the case. A town not too far away is Chillicothe, and that name means the place where the head chief over lesser chiefs had his home. And those arrowheads may have been made or used in the quick mud area, likely part of a hunting party since from ancient times there have been a long history of hunters throughout the area. To a certain extent there have also been fishing parties for ever so long, the entire area was once so full of life that between the vegetation and the animals and fish of the region, it would have been an attractive place for living or for passing through on the way to somewhere else. A place to stock up on food and furs maybe even for trade if there was more than the people themselves needed.

Once in a great while I would be in some woods and wandering around to see what I could see, inside the darker, cooler regions within the woods it was sometimes hard to walk very far because of all the weeds and brush without any path to go through, so that either go around it or figure a way through it, all the while hearing birds and other noises common to that environment. Deep inside the woods is a very noisy place though it doesn't seem so loud and jarring as anywhere outside the woods. But on a few occasions while working my way through the undergrowth and getting my legs all scratched by thorns of some of the plants, I would come to a large clearing. It was always a wonderful surprise to see that! Especially if it were a sunshiny day, after all the time getting through the darker wooded area to come out into broad daylight like that. Grass grown tall and wild, butterflies and hummingbirds galore, it really was a place I could just have stayed for a while. But usually on an errand to find some of the edible plants I had learned, it was only a short time that could be spared to enjoy the clearing. I don't know how common clearings are. Those I saw seemed to be there naturally, because I didn't notice any signs of trees having been cut down or any other evidence that people had made the clearing. But once I left it, I couldn't find it again some other day. I know that because I did look for it, in one woods after another. Anyway I'm glad I had those experiences. Always they happened when I was alone. Sometimes those pretty places turned up in my stories that I was always playing when I was young, then I was always writing down when I was older.

Daddy wasn't mechanically inclined. Like I am not mechanically inclined. Still, he fixed his own vehicles. Tractors, pick ups, cars, big semi's, any time things broke down he just did his best. Good thing he was familiar with those things because often the winch truck or the big truck would break down deep inside the woods where nobody could even see or hear that help was needed.

After my brother Paul went to the Air Force I started going with Daddy to the woods. I was 12 when he taught me to drive the winch truck across dried ruts in the dirt. Some of those ruts were deeper than others because different weight trucks had made impressions in the mud, and then when it dried, was very like cement. Now think of crossing a series of curbs of different dimensions and know the ride was bumpy enough to take me off my seat and hit my head on the roof of the cab in the truck I was driving. Still, stops and starts like that, I shifted gears and ended up going where I was supposed to end up. That was quite an accomplishment for such a novice as I was! Daddy would direct everything, but when I worked with him he constantly explained what we were doing, and why things were to be a certain way. So I would say I understood his business because of working alongside him as well as listening to his details. Besides, I was very worried about him just then, how defeated he was after Paul left. So I tried to step up and fill a need while also keeping an eye on him in case he should get hurt and I needed to go for a doctor or something.

In the first part of the job Daddy would go somewhere to look over standing trees. Maybe in somebody's yard, or maybe out in between farmer's fields, wherever he happened to go. Because there were trees everywhere. Only he was looking for walnut trees. With finely etched bark that looks like the outside of the rind of a muskmelon. Preferably growing straight and tall with some room around it for laying it down safely.

When he found something he liked, he would find out who owned that property and go see them about buying that standing tree. If they liked his price they would take the money and that is when I would go to work with him. We started with a big breakfast after the morning chores were done. I filled up his 5 gallon water bucket with ice and topped it off with water. Mama put together as many sandwiches as there were leftover biscuits and eggs from breakfast, and put those into an empty bread wrapper. Some pieces of leftover cake, or else more biscuits with honey or jam on them, into another bread wrapper. Those and the water bucket were our lunch for while we were out in the woods. When it was lunch time we would find a nice shady spot and sit down on a rock or tree stump in the shade, eat our sandwiches, drink plenty of water out of our collapsible metal cups that were always kept in the winch truck, then back to the task at hand. My dad was in his 50's then and I was an energetic child of 12. But every day I worked with him I fell asleep in the truck going home from the woods. Most times I skipped supper because I needed to go straight to bed. Daddy could work and work and work! He did the night chores, ate his supper, spent time with the rest of the family whoever was there, then went to bed. Though I had more sleep than he did, and though I was a lot healthier than him, those walnut log days exhausted me.

His method of working the walnut trees was to walk all around the tree he had in mind. Looking at all angles, much like playing pool would be, he would decide where to lay that one down. Then I was told where to stand, and I better not move from that area until he said it was safe. I was an obedient child as a rule, but when his voice took on a certain tone it froze me in my tracks and I just stayed there until he said I could move. So I had a view of everything he did at that point, because watching him work was a real lesson.

He took his gasoline powered chain saw and made cuts into the bark. It looked entirely vertical but it angled inwards at the center. When he was satisfied with that wedge he went to the opposite side of the tree and started making a horizontal cut that headed straight for the middle of that wedge. Then I could smell that good tree smell and hear the chain saw above all else. Finally there was the start of a cracking sound, the saw was turned off, and the cracking grew louder as the tree leaned into the wedge. Some time went by as it sort of wiggled back and forth but then in a boom it fell to earth. He could position it in the best possible location and if all went well, it wouldn't land halfway up into another tree. That would be the very worst thing but he could solve the problem if he needed to. Usually it just fell into a clearing.

Once the tree was on the ground I was able to move. It was incredible how big the tree was! Then taking a piece of chalk and his metal ruler, he measured a few inches more than 8 feet and made a mark. Then he measured another 8+ feet, marked it, and so on until he came to the leafy branches. Some of these were thick and long enough to mark just the same way. Maybe the whole measure and mark work took as much as half an hour. Depending on how tall the tree was, it would cut up into so many logs and these logs would be moved with the winch, and set down on the bed of the semi. That part of the work took some hours to load and then chain down the load, finally we would drive the semi out. I didn't drive the big truck at all. It was just nice to sit in the seat beside Daddy while we took the load to the mill. As ever, he had many things to say and so conversation was another lesson I learned from him. Or rather, the listening part of that. I learned to listen about the same time I learned to drive.

There was a mill he liked in St. Joseph. If he had good walnut it always went there. And when I say "good" I'm talking about veneer. Because logs are cut for a variety of uses, the use that paid most was for thin slices of perfect straight walnut to be used as gun stocks and on fine furniture. So when the walnut was of that quality, it went to that mill. The mill was owned by a man named Mr. Duncan.

It took at least an hour to drive all that way. On our way into town we had to pass the Wonder Bread bakery where the smells of fresh warm bread nearly made our mouths water. Then on to the seedy part of town where the mill was located, a series of rough dirt roads, and then finally into the yard of the mill. There was a really long driveway and we had to wait our turn to move on towards the buildings. If there were lots of trucks ahead of us we might spend the whole rest of the day in that line as we waited for loads to be checked and then unloaded.

There was a foul mouthed little man named Punk who checked all the logs. If he didn't like the whole load he would reject it and that truck would pull out of line and leave, its driver always red in the face for the cussing he'd just taken. Or else Punk might like some of the logs so he would accept those he wanted and dismiss the rest of the load. The good logs would be taken off by winch to wait in one or other of the piles of logs outside the building, Punk would write something on his pad, tear off a page, and hand it to the driver. The driver would then go into the building to get paid. Then he would drive away with some money and some logs, which he could then take to another mill who took less quality logs than the Duncan mill did

Daddy tried to fill a whole load for the Duncan mill. It was time effective to make one long day at the best paying mill, than it would be to go over there for a few logs, then drive to another town to hope to sell some other logs, maybe even elsewhere to another mill after that one.

Daddy could spot veneer quality while that tree was still standing, and he could estimate how many logs would come from that one tree. Usually it was more than 1 truck load but that was okay. The next day's work would be shorter because it would only be winching the logs on the ground onto the semi, chain them up, and drive them to the mill. For this reason his first choice of tree was always the veneer quality. He'd worked with the Duncan mill for many years and had a high opinion of Mr. Duncan. He liked Punk's knowledge but he didn't like the cussing. So Punk talked nice to my dad. He didn't pull that same trick with any of the others, as far as I ever saw.

One day we got to the mill in the early afternoon and the entire long driveway was full of trucks waiting their turn. So we pulled in behind the last one. We could see Punk walking down the line talking to the drivers. Some of them got out of the line and just turned back the way they came. Finally he came to us, he said, "Hacker, what are you doing at the end of this line? Get on up to the front!" We didn't know what that was all about but as we passed the other trucks they all gave us a dirty look. They were probably going to be stuck in that line the whole rest of the day so no more money could be made that day. And here we were, jumping to the front because Punk said so.

At the front of the line Daddy got out and talked to Punk while another man did the measuring of the logs. He measured the diameter as well as the length, put those numbers onto a pad, and when that was done, handed the pad to Punk for approval. As Daddy told Punk about his logs and his life, it was measured. If there was any question on measurements, Daddy wanted those to be re checked for accuracy. But Punk just told the man, "Whatever Hacker says it is, it is." And then he gave Daddy the paper, and Daddy went into the office and came back out with his pay. Which was cash, by the way.

As we left, Daddy told me what that whole day was about, and I was prouder of my dad than I ever had been before. Because I saw how he was treated by Punk and others, it made my head swim to see he was so respected! This sweet, sickly, sad man beside me, the one I worried over during his depression over Paul, was a man other men could only try to imitate. Because he set such a high standard for himself, not because he was ever in competition with anyone else.

The back story on that long line of trucks was that all those drivers had cut their logs short. An inch or two less than 8 feet long meant sometimes they could get more logs. But these logs were already sold as veneer. The orders for Mr. Duncan's lumber had come to him, he was buying logs to fill those orders, and all of them were then sent out by trainloads of lumber, to the manufacturing places that had bought them. But at the factory where that lumber ended up, the specs of their machinery was that they could only work with a length of 8 feet. Any shorter than that, the board wouldn't fit and couldn't be used for anything at all. Yet the factory had paid veneer prices to Mr. Duncan. Which left the mill looking like a shoddy supplier. Naturally the lumber went right back to him. Seeing that it was unusable for anything due to length, he had to accept all that lumber and pay back those who had bought veneer. He took such a loss because he was so proud of having a good reputation, and because he had a son in college who would someday inherit that mill, and because he had worked so many years to build up his reputation. But woe to those drivers who came after that day, with their little cut shorts. There was no way for them to regain their reputations. They made a couple of high sales but the rest of their work would be thoroughly checked ever after that.

Which is what Daddy knew about veneer. The machine specs called for 8 feet so he gave it a little more just in case of any turns in the wood.

And if he said the log was 8 feet, Punk knew it would be a little over but never under. Which is why when we left, dirty looks from the other drivers didn't matter a bit. As he explained all this to me, he made sure to underline the value of always doing the right thing. Honesty was for business as much as it was for private use. And it would never come back to bite, which is more than all those drivers could say for what money they'd dishonestly taken from Mr. Duncan.

Then years went by. Mr. Duncan died without warning. Young Mr. Dan Duncan had been working at the mill learning his father's business. But even his own son didn't know the many things Mr. Duncan had done among that community. He'd made a private loan to my dad and Daddy told him about that loan, and his previous payment arrangements. So that Mr. Duncan also got off to a good start with my dad.

When at the age of 79 Daddy passed away, though he had been in a 2 year hospital stay, many of his former associates heard about it. It was a very well attended funeral, so I hear. I wasn't there for the funeral. Instead, we all chose to go to Missouri in May when Daddy called us to him. Because we could only do that once, we all talked it over and decided to go in May, then not to go back when the funeral happened. Which was October of 1985. But it was said to me that he left such a long shadow by his business dealings, and I do believe that was his largest circle of influence. Those of us who knew him privately could say the same thing, as a person to set the standard for the rest of us because we always saw he was actually right. Hard as that was for me to swallow, Daddy really was always right. At least in those things he taught to me.

IN CASE I'VE FORGOTTEN THESE DETAILS

The 40 acres that straddled old Highway 6 just 2-½ miles northwest of Winston, was purchased for $4000. With a gas station on it, and nothing else. Over the next couple of decades a number of improvements were made to the property. A new house was built. Across the road a new barn was built. Back behind the hill of that barn a big pond was dug. At the southeast behind the house a smaller pond was dug. A cistern was put in beside the house but they never did find water to dig a well. Though Grandpa Parton witched for water, and several attempts were made, it was basically a dry piece of property until rain or snow hit it. It was also right in the line of tornadoes but none of those ever touched down at that place. They certainly drenched us all as they passed on by, however. So when the interstate highway went through the area on its way to connect Des Moines, IA to Kansas City, MO, they bought the entire property for $80,000. That way they had total choice of where to put the highway, and then gave the rest of the property back to the folks. They ended up taking a slice through the eastern edge going towards the southwest. So a little triangle remained on the far northeast of the property, and that piece fronted the highway. This part became rental property for a gas station. If you were to go there today you might see behind that gas station a race track. Like we used to hear ads on the radio saying Sunday Sunday Sunday, it provides entertainment and some employment for the area, but that has all come about more recently. When we lived there the entire country was farmland.

Some of the farm families near us had lots of boys. This was the goal to have plenty of boys for all the work and creating an inheritance to keep property within the family. But since there was only one boy in our family the rest of us had to step up at planting and harvest time, get up on that little red Allis Chalmers tractor, and do what had to get done. Daddy said there was money to be made in farming but it couldn't be profitable while also paying off half a million dollars' worth of fancy new equipment payments. While some farmers had very modern tractors and other equipment, Daddy just kept repairing the old ordinary tractor we'd always had. It was dependable even in its old age. Like the refrigerator they put into the house when it was built, and used it the next 20 or so years. Stuff was once made for this lifetime and maybe on into the next, so that people might inherit a working piece of equipment that would do its same job for the next generation. I doubt that time will ever be seen again but at the time we hardly thought about it at all. We just expected machines to do what they did for as long as we needed them.

Among our neighbors was the Lee family. They had lots of boys but hardly any land. So what they did, borrowed money from the bank and bought a brand new fancy tractor, and then combine, and so forth until that family owned every modern convenience a farmer could dream of having. And then they went around talking to people like my dad. He had some land but not the fancy, fast equipment. So a sort of partnership was formed between him and the Lee boys. They would come over with their equipment, plant the fields in whatever he wanted, then come back and tend the fields, and at the end they came in with just one man and a fancy machine to harvest the crops. What had taken every relative and hired day worker we could come up with, long days on end of excruciatingly hard work just the year before, suddenly was done for us by all the Lee equipment, with only one of the Lee boys doing the driving of whatever it was. Then when the harvest was in, half went to Daddy and half went to the Lees, so they could use it or sell it as they pleased, and we could do the same. What Daddy's half covered was all his animals' winter feed, seed for next year's crops, and the rest was sent to the market. So he made some money on top of getting all his needs covered, while he and the rest of us were free from the work that took so that he could go to the woods where his main income was made, and we could continue doing what we needed for ourselves.

It was during that time that I started babysitting for my sister Joanne. So from the time I was about 10. It was many years later that I found out that other people got paid to do that work. I didn't get paid. I just got told do this, do that, no money ever came my way. Until I was 14, that is. That summer my sister Maxine got me a bus boy job at the restaurant where she worked, the Rambler in Cameron. So when I did have money of my own, after so many years of working anyway, finally having a payday was extremely liberating. I loved having my own money and doing whatever I wanted with it! I bought some clothes for myself and the rest I used on Christmas gifts for the entire family. I loved having money, the concept of getting money in exchange for my work, the idea of doing my best in return for the freedoms that money brought to me, well I wouldn't ever want to make that situation stop. I know lots of people take a different view of working for a living but for me, that was my biggest turning point of all. I was able to do any variety of really ordinary work, and do it well. It brought a payday with it, and that was the biggest thrill! So far I'd worked at plenty of tasks but now all of a sudden it turns out somebody was interested in paying me to do what they needed. What a concept! It was my pleasure to have my own money. I spent some, saved some, paid whatever bills came up as a result, and made all those decisions by myself. I was empowered by that.

But back to that farm property. Once the highway paid, the folks started looking for a house in town. They found one they liked in Gallatin. So the house where they'd lived all that time was left vacant and was soon rented to a local family. At that time there was a 2 story garage next to the house, many trees, some swings for the children, and 2 ponds, a barn, and all the fields. But just the house was rented. Daddy kept his same arrangement with the Lees and then all his half was able to be sold since he'd sold off his livestock and no longer needed to provide the following year's seeds for planting.

Then there was a fire and that house burned to the ground. While the renters were away, I believe. Anyway no one was injured but the house was completely gone. So when the folks wanted to move back to the farm, they sold the house in Gallatin and put up the modular that was put up at the top of the hill on the north side of the highway. So, just like Deuteronomy chapter 28, everything my dad touched turned to profit. He lived the life he advocated, and raised his children by being the example. He gave to those in need, both in money and in opportunity since he would give anybody a job who came to him looking for work. He wasn't at all generous though. He treated people the way he wanted to be treated. To him, that's what the Bible was all about. The golden rule still holds its weight. And so far hasn't been outlawed at all. But if he was just saying one thing but doing another, I would have known that in an instant. Because I did look for that. I never found it. He really believed in honesty and integrity and in all ways doing the right thing, caring for the unfortunate as need arose, like when someone in town had a house fire and they were left out in the cold winter without anything. We gave food from our pantry. Other people gave blankets or just whatever they might have to spare. Nobody had to suffer but the entire community contributed in that way so that people could rebuild their lives after a disaster like that of a housefire. So it was what he did, rather than what he said, that I was watching and paying attention to. I found him even in his most private moments to be genuine in all the things he'd told me. And that one thing right there is more rare than I would have imagined! It truly was an honor to be his child. Other people thought we were rich and in a way we were. Only not in dollars though there were plenty of those as well. Enough money in fact that he could buy a brand new Buick on one payday. Which he did do twice. He had a black 1952 Buick and then traded it for a 1954 maroon Buick. We went in both of those cars when I could lay completely out on the back seat just like it was my own bed, on vacation up and down Highway 66. That seems so vintage, doesn't it? We drove for as long as he pleased, passing all the sights along the way, with always a motel and its swimming pool and neon lights to stay when he was tired of driving. And reptile gardens to tour. And hot dog stands, coca cola for 5 cents a bottle, I Love Lucy being a brand new tv show. And then going west on Highway 66 until finally turning around and going back. We might be gone a few days, or a week or so, and then go back home. That was a vacation we took several times. Another time we drove to Denver, stayed in motels along the way, then came home. Daddy was always so happy to get home. I was always so happy to leave it. Isn't that something?

MAMA'S STORY

My mother was just the best mother that ever was! She worked long and hard, thought of creative ways to stretch what was on hand to meet what was needed, and all the time she talked to me or else sang. She loved me so very much that I never needed another mother my whole life. She nurtured me as much as I could wish, drove me all over the country to take me to piano teachers, and then paid them in loose change that she'd been saving. She gave me that good start in life that everyone expects a mother to do, but mine did it better than any of her peers. I have been critical of some of her behaviors but that was wrong of me. Women of her generation had so much more requirements put on them. Suffice it to say, what was expected of her was beyond anyone's abilities, yet she did come up to excellence in everything she did. It's entirely to her credit that she did all that without being perfect! She never needed to be perfect but she came as close to that as possible.

On 22 Sept 1906 outside the little town of Maysville in DeKalb County, Missouri, Maud Alta Parton was born to Thomas Eugene

Parton and Nellie Maud (Fales) their second child. There was already a year old boy and the next baby coming roughly every year for the next 15 years.

Maysville was the county seat. That meant its courthouse was the center of the town, and the courthouse was put at the center of the square. There would also have been a bandstand somewhere on that square. Volunteer musicians got together for practice through the week and performed free public entertainment on most pleasant Saturday afternoons. I say pleasant because in tornado alley they do have to keep an eye on the sky all summer long. When weather permitted, people came to town to do their weekly grocery and miscellaneous shopping, and these outdoor entertainments were a nice little break from the long hard week that everybody had in those times. Sousa himself was still alive and composing in 1906. His works had such enduring popularity that even in my childhood Stars and Stripes was always played at 4th of July festivities. That music makes me think of an ice cream shop and fireworks, people in band uniforms, playing for a long time while we walked through town. This would have been part of Mama's entire childhood because these events happened in every county seat and other small towns through the area. Maybe it was a midwestern thing, or else maybe it was widely done all over the country.

In 1906 Teddy Roosevelt was president. Most people went around on foot or horse and buggy rides. Lots of people knew how to ride a horse. There was even a stable in town where you could rent a horse if you needed one. Women had so much to do at home that they seldom got out to see the sights. So Saturday shopping and concerts were prized occasions. And women didn't have the vote for almost another 20 years.

Like both her parents, Maud attended a one room schoolhouse walking distance from the family's one room house on the rented farm just east of town. There was one teacher who taught all 8 grades of local students. If a farm child could finish 8 grades of school, that was quite an accomplishment! But there were some who did that very thing. Maud wasn't one of them. She had chores at home and could seldom get away to attend school. By the time she'd finished 3rd grade her duties were such that she could no longer go to school. But her favorite brother Tommy, the next youngest after her, would tell her everything he'd learned as soon as he came home from school. He shared his knowledge with her.

Mama had one story of Christmas in her childhood. She woke up on Christmas Eve and saw her mother traipsing all around the room in her nightgown and barefoot, humming Christmas songs and obviously enjoying herself. She was filling their stockings. All the children had hung one of their own socks not some decorative thing but an actual sock of theirs. So Grandma was putting an orange down into the toe, and then filling the rest of the sock with peanuts in their shells. And she was eating peanuts as she did that. This was the only present the children would get. But Mama was surprised to see Grandma was the one who did it, not Santa Claus as she had always thought. This is when she decided she'd never lie to a child of hers, and true to her word, she made sure none of us believed in Satan Claus.

I have read a few things about Christmas celebrations long ago. James Whitcomb Riley was a poet and writer who talked in little kid stumbling vernacular. He was born into a wealthy family more merchant than farmer class, and he was actually still alive when my parents were born. He talked of Santa bringing bells and whistles for him and his siblings. But mostly he remembered eating his mother's mincemeat pies! Apparently they had mincemeat pies for any special occasion and it wasn't even a nasty thing to him. I've had my mother's mincemeat pies which I always thought she just made the recipe up to use whatever leftovers, as I know she was inclined to do. But the ones she made were meat, pieces of meat I tell you, with some raisins and other leftover kind of things, and then SUGAR all put into a pastry and baked like a normal pie would be. Imagine then the surprise that came across my mouth at first taste, what I was expecting it to be, versus what it in fact was, and this was never a special occasion memory of mine. But for James Whitcomb Riley he remembered it fondly. I can't get over that!

I think Mama didn't have an actual Christmas tree in the house, which is all for the best. The only decoration I've read and that I expect may be more like Civil War times, was just a bunch of real candles. An open flame, lots of them of course, on a piece of firewood which basically is what the tree would be by that time, though maybe it was only in place for Christmas Eve and then removed promptly the next day. That may look charming in pictures but is such a safety issue that everyone in the Parton house should have been grateful that they didn't have. And by Grandma putting an orange in each stocking, she at least didn't leave anybody out. And she gave them the one expensive thing that they never had at any other time. Peanuts were common though. Those grow easily in Missouri and probably lots of other places as well. So to use them as filler, it must have been pleasant for all 11 of those children to wake up and find. And that is maybe the one thing I can take pride in that grandma for doing since it was all about the children and not designed to get attention for herself. By pretending the Santa figure, maybe she was doing what her parents had done for her. Or else, like me, she was doing what she always wished her parents had done.

On the subject of Christmas past, as I seem to be dwelling on how much that whole thing has changed, I read the description of the last Christmas held in the Confederate white house. They didn't call it their White House. It was just The Manse. Because it's such a human story, I'm putting it in here. Not because I have any pro confederate opinions at all. At the time Abraham Lincoln was having his hands full and no easy days in that either. But the south was losing the war badly by December of 1864.

In the Richmond, Virginia area there was an orphanage run by one of the churches. Those children never had anything at all, so deprivations the rest of the southerners were feeling didn't even register in their lives. There was nothing. No food, no money to speak of, and basically worthless currency anyway. But they did firmly expect their president and his wife to provide them a nice Christmas. And so it was, because of those expectations, that Verina Davis put it all together. She and some of her lady friends searched through their children's toys to find any unused or discarded or broken things that could be repurposed.

She mentioned what some of those toys were but all I remember was a doll with no eyes. So the women did their repairs and sewed new clothes for the dolls, and a slave in the Davis house built a wooden doll's house that was so nice they used it as the grand prize award. So presents were provided. But still that left the matter of some sort of food to serve, and this is where the hard part began.

Robert E. Lee was somewhere close by with an army, and he was the one the people loved. They did not love Jefferson Davis, the president. He was just a Washington politician whose first wife was the daughter of former president Zachary Taylor. When he'd married her they went somewhere for their honeymoon, and both of them got sick. She actually died but he recovered. So they were only married for 2 or 3 months. And he had occasional bouts of sickness the whole rest of his life. Which is what makes me think of malaria, but I don't know if that was the cause.

Besides his aloof ways, and sometimes sickness he also had a rare nerve condition where all the nerves in his face were inflamed so that he was in constant pain. Under those circumstances it's hardly odd that he wasn't a nice person to be with. But he and Verina had 6 children together so there must have been some happier times. Anyway only one of those children outlived her, so there were also many tragic times in the Davis house.

But at that December a farmer had harvested 4 wagonloads of sweet potatoes. That was an enormous amount of food but there was no way to market them. So the farmer took those wagons to Lee and his men, to help with the growing starvation problems everyone was seeing. But Lee accepted 3 of the loads on behalf of his men, and told the farmer to take 1 wagon to the Manse and give it to Jefferson Davis. So that's what the farmer did. Only because Lee told him to, not because he wanted to give anything to Davis. I find that more telling than all the rest, really.

So there they were, getting the Manse all ready for the day the orphans would come for Christmas, when the farmer pulled up with a whole wagonload of sweet potatoes. The cook put together whatever there was, and possibly even mincemeat pies though that's almost more cruel than being in the south while they were losing their old men and little boys on the battle field and starving to death after Sherman's march on top of everything else. But there was no mention of mincemeat so hopefully the children were spared that experience.

Anyway they had the children come to the house. Presents were given to each orphan, though there was no mention of presents for the Davis children. And then the prize wood doll's house was awarded to the girl who was best behaved. She took her prize and sat beside it, just looking at it and not even touching it. Her award, her own property, her Christmas that included something to eat and being in the home of people who knew hospitality so well, no doubt she would always remember that day fondly. Even Jefferson Davis came to the party and was nice to everyone. But mostly it was Verina Davis who made that all happen. Just 4 months later when Lee surrendered and her husband took off in the night for Texas to avoid trial for treason, the she and her children moved to New York City. She spent the rest of her life living there in a Yankee city so different from Richmond and all the war years, but so much like her life before and after that war. She was a society lady, after all.

So the only presents mentioned were repaired toys and one exquisitely made for the occasion by someone who was soon to be free. We don't even have his name, sadly. But a valiant effort for all the people who put on a Christmas for the children of the orphanage in spite of all that was happening around them.

Another story Mama told was of their well-to-do Fales aunt and uncle who came in their own car. It caused such a stir! And all the children got to get inside, as there was no roof to the thing, and the aunt said, "Kids, hold on to your hats." and their uncle drove crazy fast like 20 miles an hour, blowing their hair around and making them all squeal with delight. Just the one time they were taken for a ride, so evidently they didn't see those relatives often, or else it was too much noise on their part so no further invitation was given. I don't really know. It could have been either way.

Mama used some strange things in her daily housework. The area of personally owned appliances changed so much from her childhood until mine, and even more in the years since I was a child! For instance, laundry and all the things that chore involved; beating clothes on a rock and running them across a washboard using a bar of homemade lye soap, that was her earliest stories of clothes washing. She didn't have to do that part because her mother did it. This all happened at the little stream near to the house. Clothes were then rinsed in the stream and draped across bushes to dry. With the parents and 11 children, that was a big load of laundry. The only thing that may have made it at all possible was that nobody had very many sets of clothes. Two outfits suitable for wearing out in public and two for doing the dirty work that farm people do much of the time. Then a lot of underclothes just because this was the most necessary of all garments. When one child outgrew their clothes the next youngest child would wear them, and so forth until either they ran out of younger children or else the fibers all fell apart from the lye and scrubbing. If there were no more younger children, any outgrown clothes would be given to near relatives, if any. Then failing any more little children's needs, any fabric still good and sturdy would be cut up to make patches for those things getting the rips and tears from normal use. And other pieces of cloth would be used in quilts or at the lowest end of their usefulness, ripped into thin strips, braided, and turned into rugs. People needed to get out of a warm bed and touch a rug before they could get their shoes on because hardwood floors got awfully cold in the chill of a winter overnight temperature fall. In the times when no fire was burning overnight, their mother got out of bed, made the first fire of the day, and while the house was heating, got started on breakfast. This was the way everybody did it at the late 1800's and early 1900's.

Once the clothes were washed and dried, the next step was ironing. It started by taking a bottle like a coke might have come in, putting a sprinkler head on it, and sprinkling the dried clothing. Just a bit of dampening over all, then each piece was rolled up and placed inside a pillow case to wait its turn on the ironing board. A pot of water was put on top of the wood burning stove and starch powder was added once the water got hot enough. When it thickened it was used to stiffen parts of garments. Like collars and cuffs. While waiting on the starch to thicken, a piece of heavy iron was put on the stove to get hot. It was shaped like an oval but with the ends very pointed. There was a dip in the top and a bar that went across the dip.A sort of door handle was used to fit that bar and make it possible to move the hot iron around on the clothes. Because the iron was always moved so it wouldn't burn the cloth, and kept at that job until the garment was dry. Another tool that looked like a long hook was used to lift the iron off the stove and put the next one on. Because every family had many irons. They were used to smooth out the wrinkles but only so long as the iron held its heat. Then it had to be replaced by a hot one. And heavy, did I mention? A little girl wouldn't be able to lift it, much less slide it around on the fabric. But when she was big enough for that task, Mama took over the ironing while her mother did other work. As you can see, keeping the house and grounds and all the people in it, without electricity or running water took many hours and many people to accomplish. With such a big family, laundry had to happen 3 or 4 times a week. (This is how it was done when Mama was a child. Naturally, being a thoroughly modern woman, she had a wringer washing machine to cut those chores down in the amount of time they took, but only after she was married.)

Meals were cooked on the kitchen stove, with its four removable flat lids moved with that same long hook as the irons needed. Pots of food boiled on top. Inside that stove was a small rectangular box for an oven, and just below that, the fire box. It took a lot of experience to cook and to bake, especially, when temperature wasn't controlled but food just variously placed around the fire.

So the fact that Mama learned to bake biscuits when she was still too little to iron clothes, has to be among the hardest things to do well. She did that so well! No doubt there were some disappointments and burnt food in all that learning, but what came of it was that she learned to feed an entire room full of people on the produce and stored items easily at hand. All her life she cooked like that. Never less than a dozen people per meal, but there were more and more leftovers as less people came to the table. She was famous in the neighborhood and among family farther away as well, for her wonderful cooking. She could take a live chicken from the hen house and before long have it frying and sending that smell straight to our noses and tastebuds started responding. Then a few fresh vegetable out of her massive garden, some pickles she'd made a while ago, a batch of biscuits into the oven near the end of the cooking, and served all up hot from the stove. Honey and homemade butter for the biscuits if you could wait that long, or else eaten without them as soon as they cooled a little. Iced tea in summer, or sometimes lemonade, a bowl of strawberries or any fresh fruit to round up all the food groups just like that, and then a sliver of what was left of gooseberry cobbler or rhubarb pie, anything that wasn't mincemeat. Though mincemeat pies made an appearance occasionally. Southern comfort food it was. Fried chicken, fried vegetables, white flour, sugar, you know. All the stuff we are taught not to eat. But it certainly was a delight to have something she cooked.

For making clothes, there was one labor saving device, a Singer sewing machine that was powered by a treadle. I never could learn to work a treadle but Mama learned on that kind of machine. Her feet worked the treadle up and down, as she guided the fabric through the process. She was always using 3-in-1 Oil, that was the name of it, and it came in a sort of flask can with a pointy top. She would stick it into the machine and squirt some oil across the inner workings, and never did that oil migrate onto her fabric. It almost wasn't even the same process as I've used all my life!

It was important that work be done during daylight hours, inside the home as well as outside. But for the dark, they used kerosene lamps. That might be early in the evening, or early in the morning, or any time it was too cloudy dreary to see what you were doing. So a supply of kerosene was kept far from all heat sources. Those kerosene lamps had a bowl where the kerosene was put, then a wick went between the kerosene and the smaller neck of the lamp, ending up in a holder so that it could be rolled up farther and farther. That is the part that was lighted. The fire it created danced across the walls in the most other worldly shapes. It was nearly impossible to read by kerosene light because the light was so sporadic as it was. But for other things, it did put out a good amount of light. But stink? Oh the smell is unmistakeable! And then at bedtime the lamps would be put out. Overnight the glass cooled so that one of the early morning chores, right after breakfast dishes were done, was that those parts of the lamps had to be removed, washed, and replaced to get the lights ready for the next evening. This was usually only done once a day and everybody had several of those lamps so sometimes they only used one or two at a time. Then it didn't take long to clean in the morning. But if company came to visit after dark, then more of the lamps would be lighted and the next morning that brought extra work that had to get done.

People used to make their own brooms using dried vegetation tied around a stick. Of course those brooms got used so often that they soon wore out and were replaced. (When Mama was married she had a carpet sweeper, ooh so fancy! A big improvement over the homemade brooms of her childhood.)

One thing that only happened a few times a year was the soap making. Mama really enjoyed making her own lye soap out of only 3 ingredients, fine ash taken out from the stove, a can of lye, and some fat. This was serious stuff so I had to keep far away. The smells of that process, and the extra care it required, meant that she made enough bars of soap to last her through several months of laundry. Any other leftover ash from cleaning out the stoves was allowed to cool thoroughly, then dumped onto the garden and spread around. I don't know if it helped the soil, but that's how it was used.

To get the soil improved, such as when you'd had a heavy crop of corn or other plant that used up the nutrients, Mama would keep a bucket of rusty nails, and some water on top of them. This was to water those parts of the garden that would need extra help. So she was adding back iron into the soil, as well as leaving the pulled weeds and cut stalks of the garden to mulch the ground they came from, to add back to the soil whatever the crop had taken out.

One thing neither of my parents ever told me about was the 1918 Spanish flu epidemic. Both of them were old enough by that time so that they would have noticed if anyone in their immediate area had died or even come down with that flu. Because they didn't tell me anything about it I doubt if they had any stories to tell. The fact that they didn't mention it persuades me that the disease was only in certain pockets of the world and that it didn't come into either of their childhood areas. Bethany and Maysville, MO is where they were when that happened. Though it started in Kansas, then moved with soldiers being transferred into Europe during World War 1, it could be that contact was just not a concern for either of them. It wasn't very far away from either of their locations but maybe wasn't carried into communities close to the starting point of that outbreak.

Speaking of Kansas, being nearly at that border there were some stories having to do with going there once in a while. When I was in high school one Sunday we happened to be taking a long drive that ended up at Lawrence, KS. Daddy thought his mother's younger brother his Uncle Willie, lived there. So we found a phone booth and I got out to look him up in the phone book. They only had a small phone book since Lawrence wasn't very big at the time. But they had an abundance of listings for Kelly as well as Kelley. So I asked Daddy which spelling it was, and he didn't know. There were a lot of listings for Will Kelly and also for Will Kelley and I spent all the dimes we had but never did find the one that was Daddy's uncle. Only in recent years have I found Grandma's obituary written by Grandpa, and he gave the spelling as Kelley. I researched William Patterson Kelley which is the name I had for Grandma's father. I found him as a young man after the Civil War, marrying Malinda Jane Snead which I am sure was Grandma's mother, and they lived for a time on a farm straight east of St. Louis. About the middle of southern Illinois. Her father had a farm there, she may have grown up there, but that entire time frame was the Reconstruction, and very little paperwork got done as far as taxes, deeds, and all that I have so easily found at other times in other places.

A BIT ABOUT FARM LIFE

I would just say a little about swine in general. They only eat as much as to make themselves full. It's easy enough to think they eat everything they come across, but that isn't their way at all. They make noise when they eat, just as chickens and cows do. But they never eat themselves to death. Dogs will, however. If a farmer wanted to go somewhere overnight could easily just set out all the food the hogs would need, and then not worry about their care. That is, if they all had nose rings.

Nose rings are inserted to stop them from using their snouts to dig out from under the fences and thus be liberated to run all over the country. But still they dig with those snouts. The rings just keep them from digging a hole big enough to make their escape.

Because there is a thick layer of fat under those tough hides, and also because they don't sweat at all, the only way a hog or even a baby pig can control their temperature is to use their snout to hollow out a sort of bed for themselves in the dirt. Then rolling over onto their backs, each one gets a dirt bath. They like it even better when those little dips in the dirt get rained on, then thick black dirt cakes their whole self with only the eyes to show from inside a mud crusted self. This is the way they like to go around, and if they didn't do that would quickly overheat and die. But this is why they have such a smelly place to live. It really stinks far worse when they are kept inside a structure. So the only house they have are these little triangle things where the mother will lay down and allow her piglets to nurse. Otherwise they just deal with the great outdoors.

Part of their world is dealing with wildlife. Mostly they hold their own with predators. Nobody can bite through those hides, that's for sure. Only their bellies are soft but all they have to do is lay down, to protect themselves. Even porcupine quills won't penetrate their hides! And rattlesnakes don't have a chance against them. They actually eat snakes if one comes close. They are so mean by nature that wolves leave them well alone. But this is why if you ever decide to get a farm, you should leave swine out of your plans. We had them for meat for ourselves of course, but mostly they were for selling. Each litter the sow will have 10 or more piglets, which if the farmer puts 1 away for his family to eat, still leaves plenty to send to market when they get up to weight. Or else cut some out to breed if there are traits the farmer wants to encourage. Such as quick growth. Naturally nothing can be done about their habits. But for those who put on enough weight to be sold at market, that presents another nice payday.

Mama tended to slopping the hogs but like I mentioned, nobody went into the pen except for Daddy. I tended to driving the cattle out of the barn to their grazing pasture in the morning, then about the time the chickens went to bed I would go bring the cows back to the barn so they could be settled for the night. They spent all day eating and drinking in their patient kind of way. But cows have their different personalities so some are more gentle than others. Never make the mistake of thinking because they are so roundy that means they are also gentle. It means nothing of the sort. They weigh a ton or more, and if one of them comes at you, just get out of their way. They run pretty fast but you can outrun them. Especially if you keep going. They soon run out of steam and stop to graze some more. We had one bell cow. That was Old Mae. She was a red cow so there was a lot of Jersey in her. Or may Guernsey. Either way, her milk was the one that provided the most cream. She was born in winter, unlike most farm animals. They need to be born in spring when the weather is mild, and have most of the year to get strong enough to live through the next winter. But somehow, her mother took matters into her own hands and just had that calf in the middle of a blizzard. Maybe it was February. I was 4 years old the day Daddy brought her all wet and crying into the kitchen to dry her off. It was my first animal job, keeping her confined to that warm corner by putting chairs around her and keeping her from breaking lose.

Anyway, Old Mae was a natural mother. She had calves of her own, which is the only reason a cow gives milk at all. But she could feed her own calf and take on an orphan as well, that's how nourishing her milk was. So Daddy would buy a calf at auction to have Mae raise. Over the years we had a nice little herd of all kinds of breeds of cattle, all girls of course. Daddy didn't keep a bull but paid the neighbor for stud service. That was cheaper than feeding a bull for the whole year, plus the neighbor was compensated and so the bull was affordable for some farmer to keep.

So when I took the cows to pasture I only led Old Mae. She knew me and allowed me to boss her around, but none of the cows could boss her. She was the bell cow. The one who wore the bell, and when the others heard the bell ringing they followed after her. She knew, too, when I came over the hill to get them in the afternoon, to come to me. The entire herd came along and went into the barn, I shut them in, and that chore was done.

I actually liked the cows. They enjoyed themselves out in the pasture. Sometimes they felt like running and exercising but mostly they grazed over the grasses and went to the pond for a drink when they wanted. Also on hot summer days they would stand in the water to keep cool. They used their tails as fly swatters or people swatters, but look out when any one of them lowered their head and came toward you. That is the bovine way of attack. Their strength is in their head which, if horns are allowed to grow, they can spear a person. For that reason the horns get removed while they are little.

As for the bulls, we usually didn't keep them. They eat a lot, and besides all that, foul tempered and hard to keep. But the problem with that, the cow won't produce milk unless she's doing that for her own calf. That is called "fresh" meaning you can expect about 2 years of milk if you add a foster calf before she weans her own. That way, the milk will keep being produced for a while. Old Mae had so many foster calves over the years!

So, the husbandry part of all that is, you have to have access to a bull every so often. If you don't keep your own, then you can take advantage of different breeds and get the qualities you most want in the offspring. If you do keep your own bull, he's the only one because that's how they are set up. So after a few years, you would have some inbreeding problems and of course you can't build a good herd on that basis.

The thing to do here is to purchase stud service, and that was commonly done in that area. One farmer would keep a bull for his own use as well as provide service for some of his neighbors, and we were glad to pay that fee since it was beneficial to all parties involved. And there were several farmers who could meet the needs of the community.

Bulls, like all the bovine cousins, have their strength in their heads. Their necks are really strong, their horns are dangerous weapons, and they simply lower their heads while at the same time running full blast towards their target. If you are that target, move immediately to safety because the bull is more than a ton of murder that won't easily be stopped. The expression "taking the bull by the horns" comes straight out of this scenario. If you would get control of the bull, the only way to do that is to put your two hands firmly around the tip of each horn. Once you get in that position, you can very easily direct his movements and that doesn't even take a lot of effort on your part. But, just before you get into that position, you are most definitely in harm's way. In order to get control, you have to be so close to being run over and gored that many grown men didn't want to take the chance of owning their own bull, much less have their children in such danger. So you can see why it was to our advantage to pay the fee to those who kept a bull. So, when calves were born, the boys might be reared to sell as studs. In that case you would leave the horns intact and just sell them before they reached full maturity. Otherwise, you might want to use as beef so you would get those horns off and also go one step further, to make sure full maturity was never reached. That is a terrible process and I don't want to explain it fully just because it creeps me out. That's called castration. There is a change in behavior but still, even if they grow old, they're never really so docile as the females.

But even the females grow horns. These have to be removed because, even docile as they are, that's still over a ton of occasional violence. Even de-horned, even in old age, they will still lower their heads and run as fast as they can toward their target. It's something they do out of fear. We called that "getting spooked" and that could happen for any number of innocent reasons. No doubt in response to herd protection needs of that long ago time when they didn't live with us. But what if real danger comes to them? They don't respond in that self protective way but they just run like a trainwreck, except that they are packed together. They keep a sort of formation that way but real predators, such as wolf packs, can easily hunt them when they do that.

We never kept horses. Because my dad used machinery instead of horses for pulling plows like Grandpa did, he had little need for horses. Instead of a big drain on the food supply, those crops could then be grown that the cows could eat. Only rich people would keep horses when they didn't need them for farming. Because there were people who liked to go horseback riding, and kept their own stables for just that kind of entertainment, but we didn't know anybody like that. Still, horses were fairly common in the area. I used to see them in the sale barn. Interested buyers would be inspecting their mouths. That's because a young horse's teeth are big and an old horse's teeth are used so much on oats, that husk grain they eat, that wears the teeth down the older the horse gets. So the old saying, "Don't look a gift horse in the mouth" just means that, if somebody was giving you a horse, it would be rude for you to inspect its mouth to see how valuable it was. That would be like looking on the back of a greeting card to see how much the person paid for it, rather than just read what the card had to say. Rude.

HOUSEHOLD DUTIES

Housework before paper towels, sick days before Kleenex and how the new disposable items improved life while creating a monster in landfills. In fact, life was a whole lot ickier on your hands when there was no such thing as disposable stuff, no plastic of any kind. Sure that stuff stays in the landfills and clogs up the oceans. That's the downside of clean and convenient products. But imagine if you will, paper straws. They disintegrated into your drink if you took too long to finish it. They unraveled in a spiral, most often right in your mouth while you were sucking. Too creepy to return to those days! Before paper towels we used cloth, washed them and used them again, even cleaning out the oven and other hard uses. So of course they got big holes in them. After a while even those had to be discarded since they were used completely up. Now think of diapers and how babies and their mothers were able to carry on with all life's demands while also washing out dirty diapers. You had to have 5 dozen diapers for a newborn, and then replace some of those so another 2 dozen purchased before potty training. Of course they made wonderful cleaning cloth/furniture waxing and oven cleaning uses besides, but I never knew anyone to buy cloth diapers to use around the house. Only after they'd served their original purpose would they be reassigned to such tasks.

SOME LOCATION DETAILS I NEED TO CLARIFY

Where my Hacker grandparents lived when I was a child;
Where the Sam Hacker/Minnie (Kelley) Hacker family lived during much of my dad's childhood; unknown. It was outside the town of Bethany, MO but I really have no idea of where that was. When World War 1 ended, when that news reached Bethany, it may have been late at night on November 11, 1918. Daddy would have been 12 so likely recovered from his 2 years of sleeping on the sofa in the parlour. He told me that there was a lot of noise coming from town. So much in fact that Grandpa saddled a horse and went to see what it was all about. And when he got home he told them that the war had been ended. So that farm was near enough to town that they were disturbed in the evening, probably all sitting around after dinner, maybe talking or playing, and that the noise interrupted their activities. But I don't know what direction from town. I think the Grand River runs through the area and that is a river that always flooded out seemed like every other week, or at least fairly often. Since

there were never any stories about flooding, that farm couldn't have been close to the river. Possibly to the north, though I don't remember why I thought it was north. It seems like Daddy said something to make me think that.

Then in my lifetime my Hacker grandparents lived in a small house with a big backyard, a couple of blocks straight east of the Gallatin square. If I remember correctly, because I was at that house several times. The first time I remember being there was at night in the winter, it was just me and my parents that time, driving in the car and going to see Grandma and Grandpa Hacker. We came into the living room. Grandpa brought hard back kitchen chairs from the kitchen for my parents to sit down. There was another chair, maybe a rocking chair, and Grandma sat there. And there was a bed, and Grandpa sat on the bed. Grandma held me on her lap and she kissed me while the grownups were talking. Of course, children were to be seen and not heard, which saying I already knew by heart and I was not yet 4 years old. So I didn't talk. I don't know what they said to each other but they talked for what seemed like a long time, and then we went home. It was just a few days later when we were having breakfast, that someone came knocking on the kitchen door. It was a man. He said Grandma had passed away. My dad said "Ummmmm" so low, like a full octave lower than his usual speaking voice, his face went white, and he sat right down on the chair at the table. With the typical radar that passed between the two of them, Mama was alert to his reaction before he made it into the chair. She rushed over to him, I don't know what all else after that but later, after she'd made sure Daddy was okay, she explained to me that the Grandma who had kissed me while she talked with my parents had gone to be with Jesus in heaven. Though I remember a very many funerals, that one doesn't come to mind. I don't know if I went to it, but if my parents went then it was sure that I was also there. Because that's just how it always was.

She had died of a massive heart attack and so it was quick. She was 73 years old. Grandpa kept living in that house for some years and we went there often to see that he was doing okay. Those were the years when I went up into that cherry tree to pick cherries before the birds could get them all. But it was all kind of too much for him. He was 11 years older than his wife, still very active and not using a cane or anything. But still, it kind of all got away from him and so he sold the house and lived a short time with us. Not very long, though because he went downhill like a banana peel once he left Gallatin. Those were the times when he could barely hear anything but he could still talk a blue streak. He told me stories of his school years, how he was the class clown and made the all the girls laugh. He talked about tricks he played on some of his brothers and cousins, and always his eyes danced and sparkled when he told those stories. He had the most beautiful facial lines! When he would take a nap on the couch, even in sleep he seemed always to be smiling. The smile lines were so deep, and I wished that I might have such pretty wrinkles as that. Now of course, I do have plenty of wrinkles though they are far from pretty. Still, my wrinkles are more the shape of a smile than of a frown, so I accept that. No botox is going to interfere with that! When Grandpa got so frail that he really needed care he went into a private home where the lady of the house took in pensioners. She did provide a bedroom and meals but still, he had pneumonia which he never quite recovered from, and lost interest in food. That house was outside McFall, MO. So it ended up with him being so sick he was admitted into the hospital in Bethany. There he went into a coma and after some days passed away without ever regaining consciousness. As it happened, that was in Harrison County, where he'd been born in 1868, and then died in 1957. Though in all those years he'd lived in many other places. He was my favorite grandparent. I remember that he looked right into my eyes whenever he talked to me. It seemed that he cared about me. My brother said the same thing about him. I think he must have been everybody's favorite because all his children were specially fond of him. They each had funny memories of things he'd said and done when they were little. Anytime those relatives got together they would spend a long time talking and laughing over those memories. That is, any time they weren't having quarrels between themselves, and that was actually most of the time whenever they got together. Only when it was Aunt Janie and Daddy, that was peaceful conversation as though they each gave the other one a respect that none of the others seem to give. Uncle Charlie was also easy to get along with though never forget that he was in charge, I remember that about him. And that he looked like Grandpa Hacker must have looked at a few decades back. Same dancing sparkling eyes, a lot of smile lines, but the kind of voice that you would stop whatever you were doing when he spoke to you. My dad was the total authority in our house, but Uncle Charlie had that same way even when he was in our house. Kind of strange now that I think of it. I did like all the aunts and uncles, each in their own way. Aunt Nora was the bossy one but underneath it all she wanted my dad to to be well no matter how often he seemed so frail. Uncle Roy of course, the funniest man you could imagine, what with his great command of the argument. But he always wanted my dad to be well, just like the rest of them. They all knew what it was like to lose a sibling. And that was only a century ago!

One trait that I saw first in Grandpa Hacker and then in my dad, my siblings, my children, and grandchildren. It hasn't skipped a generation in that series of 5. My notice of it started with Sam Hacker but no doubt it came from farther back. The animation in the face and the eyes, when one of this select group is telling a story or really just talking about anything of interest to them. It really is a subtle thing and I would have missed that one entirely if I hadn't had children of my own. That's how I've been able to see such familiar expressions that call other family members to memory. I remember a look on Grandps's face while we were talking. I have always been quick at reading people's faces. It's typically something the youngest child does well, and that makes a lot of sense to me. But when he looked at me that way I couldn't figure it out at all, what that face meant. I know it now though, because I've worn the same face myself as I recoginize family expressions in the generations. Most recently I saw it in Nick. He didn't know what my look meant, I could tell. That also I remember wearing the face of not understanding. It doesn't happen all the time, that particular expressive animation of the entire face and a little bit of the body, too. But when it does, what a thing of beauty it is! Kind of like Grandpa is still making me laugh like he always did in my childhood. Or seeing my own child again at an earlier age. It is delightful. For that reason alone I'm so happy I had children to be able to pass that trait on into the future.

Where my Parton grandparents lived when I was a child; Altamont

I was still little enough that I had to have an afternoon nap even though I wasn't even tired and only a teeny bit cranky (as every little child says) when we used to spend all day over at the farm on the east side of Altamont. Mama would drive us just a little bit east of Altamont and then make a left turn down a dirt road. It was a dirt road but a wide one. There were farms along that road and this was the main way to get to each one where you would want to buy produce. The folks went to individual farms when they bought live chickens or dairy products or extra vegetables if ever those were needed. So there were some farmers along that area who they would have dealt with, and knew the quality to expect. Naturally this was all word of mouth repeat business so only the ones who had built up their reputations could make any money as a sort of side business. As well, among the Mennonnite families in particular, the women were absolutely famous for their yard goods. That stuff was tough as nails and would last for a few lifetimes whether you made it into a garment or a quilt. They did their own weaving, from their own wool and maybe they bought cotton if they wanted to make fabric of it. I don't know where they would have got supplies but I do know cotton didn't grow in that entire region. Yet, the Mennonites had fabric by the yard, and that was for their own use as well as some extra to sell. They liked solid colors, mostly black but sometimes a light or bright color sneaked in among the yardage. They also made home remedies which is where we shopped if we needed cough medicine and such as that. They knew many uses for garden plants as well as wild ones. Mama asked their advice sometimes when she needed really to see a doctor. As a little child I can remember that nobody went to a doctor unless it would be some extreme matter. I was in school when I first saw a doctor.

But the farm where we were going to visit Grandma on one of Mama's all day long cleaning and cooking for her, was off that big dirt road onto a small rutted dirt road that showed it didn't have a lot of traffic. I knew that by the ruts and how close the weeds came right up to the car as we drove along. It was almost like we had to brush against them just to get through, that's how aggressively they grew along that road. That shows fertile soil because really, weeds don't need good soil to thrive. But these weeds did far more than just survive. They were thick and tall and only a grown up would dare to walk through them. Sticker weeds galore, poison ivy and all kinds of unpleasant plants in alongside edible ones, that little environment was the ideal place for pheasants to nest and raise their young. Foxes lived in there as well though, so even at best it was a tough life for any birds who nested on the ground. I soon learned to identify pheasants because of the times we went down that road. So Mama would turn right onto the smaller road that had come out to a T along the big dirt road. We would go up and down a couple of hills and always see Grandpa out in the field walking along behind his horse drawn plow. Mama would say, "There's Poppy!" and honk the horn, he would turn towards us and wave, and we went on down the road to where a big weeping willow stood. Some wild lawn full of every flower that grew wild in the area as well as plenty of volunteers that had escaped from the garden, and thick extra green grass that cushioned my fall whenever I tried to walk through the front yard. That's how little I was when I first remember going there. Not really good at walking outside but fully able to walk on flat floors inside, so maybe I was 2 or so. While Mama fixed things around Grandma's house I listened to them talk and sometimes amused myself by playing a sort of little story in my thoughts. Likely based on some of my dreams because those were so very interesting. Full of color and strange things as well as people I knew behaving in ways I didn't expect. I think that must have been the early days of my imagination because sometimes I thought that stuff was real, other times I knew it was just pretend. Still, I could amuse myself with a story line even in the times when I still needed an afternoon nap.

I loved to play out front of the house but was never allowed to do that unless Mama and other people were there to watch over me. But when I grew a little bit older and had cousins there at the same time, we would go all the way down to that weeping willow where we could be completely out of sight from the house. That was where I played with cousins around my age, and I was the one in that group who directed the storyline of characters that they would each play. Most times it was just me, though, so I used sticks and rocks to fill out the cast of characters while I played good guys and bad guys, fabulous princess, hearty giant, or big grown up mother of lots of precious babies. So, if there were playmates or not, basically I played roles out of my stories. Much of the plot had to do with justice, I remember that so well because justice was central to all my stories. Now I think it was because I saw some instances when justice was obvious, and some other times when justice just didn't happen. I was still making my world view based on farm animals, seasonal work, and a houseful of siblings who each bossed me around in the most difficult ways. Because if I did what one person said, then another person got mad and yelled at me. As a result, often as it was possible, I learned to find a good sheltered play space and just deal with my sticks and rocks because at least they followed direction.

But inside that house is where I mostly had to amuse myself for the time we were stuck there. Grandma was always sick and the sound of children playing made her even sicker, so maybe that's why I did so much story telling just in my thoughts. I could be as loud or as quiet as anything, if it was all in my thoughts. But if it was something other people could see or hear it was a huge disturbance to them because Grandma was just so sickly. Now that I'm telling about this, clearly I didn't want to be there any more than she wanted me to be there. I can't imagine my mother couldn't read that in my face. And yet, several days a week that's what happened. And that house never looked any different next time we went there, it was all as if nobody lifted a finger while Mama wasn't there to clean and cook. She had taken that role since her early childhood but really she was capable of so much more than that. It might have been fun to know her when she was a young unmarried woman doing just what she pleased.

So that house. Let me describe it as we approached down that narrow long driveway. Big deep ruts in the dirt, clumps of weeds growing right down the middle but short because sometimes a car would come along. Mostly brown going through lush green on either side, down a hill then up, we could see the two story white/gray/weathered old fashioned house with its fancy front porch and Victorian kind of trim along the top and sides. Sometimes in summer we would sit out on that porch while Mama snapped the beans and took off those little tips and tops and threw them out to where chickens were walking around the porch. She might have brought us out a tall sweet glass of cold tea but there was no ice. She and I shared the glass of tea but Grandma had her own. But when we drove up, we didn't go to the front porch. We pulled into the turnaround behind the house between the barn and the back porch, which was all screened in and very cozy. I liked the back porch most times because the sunlight came in there so nice and warm. Then on into the kitchen which was a large open room with a cast iron cook stove where meals were prepared. There was a sort of dresser where dishes and linens were kept, and on the top of it a surface for prepping food. There was small table where up to 4 people could sit, and on the table a kerosene lamp which would be lit anytime it was needed. Usually only at night but sometimes on a stormy day, the only light they used inside the house was that kerosene lamp and there were several of those throughout the house.

There was also an upstairs where a small bed sat and that's where I was put down for a nap though I wasn't even tired. I would lie on that bed trying not to hear the wind screaming around the corners of the outside because that was such a sad and scary sound. And after a really long time I would be asleep and not able to hear that, which was my favorite part of being inside that house.

I don't remember any other rooms inside that house. Mostly I remember the yard and garden, the place where firewood was cut and stacked, the well with its hand pump, and the big barn. They didn't have livestock really, not like we did. Just Grandpa's horse that he used for field work and sometimes went for a ride on that horse, and some chickens, and then there were Grandpa's bee hives. He kept bees, collected the honey, and took care of as many hives as he needed. I don't know if he also had honey to sell but most likely he did. Primarily for their own use but any extra could be sold. That was the way for produce, eggs, dairy products, and whatever crops that grew in the fields. Grandpa may have planted corn and beans. It seems to me that I saw those in his fields. I never saw alfalfa like what my dad planted, but maybe there were fields I didn't ever see. It would be hard to imagine a farm without alfalfa, for that's where they get the hay to feed the livestock in winter. I know that in previous years Grandpa had tried his had at raising tobacco but didn't do well enough with that crop to keep doing it. So corn and beans would have been every farmer's cash crop. Sometimes watermelons were grown as cash crop. And of course garden produce could always be used in lieu of cash at certain little stores in the area. Some farmers dealt only in cash though, and that was more and more common during the prosperous times after World War 2.

Weatherby

From our driveway along the roadside on Highway 6 I stood and waited for the schoolbus. I was the first one to get on in the morning and the first one to get off in the afternoon. But as I stood waiting for the bus I could look down the road a little way and see Uncle Jimmy's children standing on the south side of the road. Across the road Uncle Joe's children waited for the bus. I was close enough to hear them talking and laughing with each other. Those were the nearest Parton cousins. A few roads to the west was the one where Grandma and Grandpa Parton moved after they left the Altamont farm. Grandma was so exhausted by that move that she said she hoped never to move again for the whole rest of her life. As it happened, that was the case. But our schoolbus didn't go that far to the west along Highway 6. Instead it turned right and went in a roughly circular back roads kind of way until it came back down to Highway 6 and straight on into Winston. Most of the kids who rode that bus lived along that circular route. There were some lovely farmhouses and miles of pretty fields to look at while we went along. Always somewhere on that trip, no matter what season, could be seen the cattle out in their tight little circles, and I thought of my two sets of Parton cousins in that same kind of grouping way. I had some friends along the bus route but I never went to visit them at their home. Instead, we laughed and talked at school. So my interaction with the entire community was carried on at school, with chores that had to get done after school. Other than that, with my parents and siblings, I went to church on Wednesday nights and Sunday mornings. Also with my immediate family I went to Grandma and Grandpa Parton's house several times a week year round, but most lengthy and even most interesting were Thanksgiving and Christmas. Thanksgiving was the best of those holiday huge days of eating with the grownups and playing with the cousins. Because it was normally nice enough to eat outside, long tables were set up across the entire backyard so that we could all sit down together. Ten of their children, along with spouses, already makes a group of 22 besides the parents. And each of Mama's siblings had more children than she did. There were only 5 of us in my immediate family, which now seems like a large family, but at the time we were the smallest family in that backyard. I estimate I must have 100 cousins but really, I have no idea how many there were. I do know that of all my uncles, there were lots of Parton children and each one of them was wanted. There are no stories among my people of a boy getting a girl pregnant and then leaving the area just to avoid taking care of a baby. No, they wanted each child. So it was typical when I was growing up that everybody lived in a 2 parent home. Some lived in really poor homes, but still there were 2 parents taking care of them And when we were all at school, the teachers could exercise that Supreme Court kind of authority by saying to us, "I will send a note to your father" if the class was getting too rowdy to pay attention or some kind of bad behavior. Of course nobody in their right mind would want their father to hear of those things, and so we all sat straighter at our desks and dropped the attitudes that teachers didn't like. And I, among all the kids in class, had my own standard when it came to my dad finding out how naughty children in general could be. It had come into my mind long before I ever went to school, that my dad had such pretty eyes, and that he used them to communicate with everyone. I never wanted to look into those eyes and see that he was disappointed in me. That would have been an unbearable thing. And so it was my priority that I would never allow myself to behave in a way, even far from his presence, that would make him be disappointed in me. And I'm thankful to God to say that for the entire next 40 years that I knew him, I never did see that in his eyes. I did see his disappointment in other people, though. So it would be easy to spot. One other thing I never did see, was that my dad told me one thing yet acted exactly the opposite. I looked for that but it never did happen. And so, I came to understand that his words were honorable. Like the person he was. I could count on him whether he promised to punish me or reward me. That little piece of understanding was the very base I grew on. As an adult I went looking for "truth" and as a result, behaved in many stupid choices and did many stupid things. But then I came back to his truth which was never hidden from me that whole time. And even though he knew I wasn't perfect, he still never looked at me with disappointment in his eyes. Instead, he was proud of me, that I had grown up to surprise him with my work and other such things that he really did admire. In summary, he was always on my side no matter what. He expected all his children to act in an honorable way, and if we needed a spanking we would get it but for almost all my childhood I had nothing to fear from my dad. So long as teacher didn't send him a note, that is.

GENERALIZATION OF THE 1950'S ERA IN THE MIDDLE OF AMERICA

It was the time of Made In America labels on quality goods. That was nearly a guarantee of long years of use no matter what the item that wore the label. Cars from that time kept on going for decades after. My parents only ever had one refrigerator in that house on Highway 6. Maytag washing machines especially the wringer types, went on doing a perfect job and never really wore out entirely that I ever saw. So manufacturing jobs were the big pull that drew people to cities. Those blue collar union jobs were very well paid, packed with benefits, and promised pensions to those who stayed with them for enough years. Usually 25 or 30 years on the job would earn a gold watch and a pension for the rest of the retiree's life. And during that same era, my dad worked at many things. He was self employed. For most other men though, they worked at many things after they got home from their day job. So it was a tremendous generation of super hard working people, many of whom had lived for part of their lives on the farm. Most mothers were the housekeepers of their home like you may remember from Leave it to Beaver and other early sitcoms. My mother did all that sort of thing. Plus she raised cocker spaniel puppies which she sold to pet stores. She bought used furniture at estate sales, reworked things, and sold or gave away to many of our neighbors and family members. She also raised a big garden, took care of chickens and sold eggs sometimes, made our clothes, and helped raise many children. It seems now that there was a kind of constant energy about those people. Though each person is unique, they all shared that work ethic. As a result, nearly every farm and small town around them had lush yards, buildings kept in good repair, and at least one car in the driveway. Often it would be an older car but carefully kept to last for many years. So prosperity was the background of my childhood. I didn't know any severe poverty areas though in big cities there were always slums. Even at that, you would see people out pulling weeds out of the flower beds, doing so many other things besides just being at work all the time. In my adult life that whole manufacturing thing was slipping but still in major areas industry supported the population around them. These days all of that is gone. For a variety of reasons, mostly because values change over time, now if anyone does have a job they have to put in so many hours just to bring home a paycheck that they may not have energy left to paint houses, or any other side jobs that were once common to the middle class.It was a wonderful time to grow up, no matter that there were so many problems alongside that kind of economic vigor. It hardly seems real any more but all that stuff did happen.

This collection of memories covers those people I knew and a little bit of those earlier ancestors, whose information was collected from researching documents. I have tried to keep it accurate but mistakes may be found in spite of my attempts. That's why I ask you to search for yourself, so that mistakes can be corrected before any future generations who are interested in this subject will have the best possible information.